THE ANATOMY (

THE ANATOMY OF A CHOICE

An Actor's Guide to Text Analysis

Maura Vaughn

University Press of America,® Inc.
Lanham · Boulder · New York · Toronto · Plymouth, UK

Library of Congress Control Number: 2010924581
ISBN: 978-0-7618-5109-7 (paperback : alk. paper)
eISBN: 978-0-7618-5110-3

To the wonderful students, faculty, and staff of the Branson School,

and to the Wood Family Fund, who made this work possible.

CONTENTS

FOREWORD

FOREWORD

MAURA VAUGHN'S *THE ANATOMY OF A CHOICE* is an indispensable handbook for any young actor starting out on their long journey to become a theatre artist. Come to that, it's a most useful tool for any actor already on that journey who should, when lost in rehearsal or performance, quickly refer to her concise, well-written advice, and learning, and they will soon find new and better avenues opening up. They will learn a lot.

Quite rightly she puts great emphasis on reading and continually re-reading the text of the play. Not only reading, but also digging, asking questions to stimulate the imagination, and so enabling the actor to bring the playwright's character to life, not allowing the actor simply to deliver a version of him- or herself. She asks for hard work and dedication: obviously, here is a director and teacher who will not settle for easy answers and sloppy results.

At the end of each of her chapters, there is a review sheet for the actor to fill in and answer, reminding them of the work they are asked to do in the preceding chapter; an invaluable tool not found in any (as far as I know) other books on acting.

Another invaluable piece of advice she gives is for the actor to black out any stage directionsin the printed script, except say, the obvious entrances and exits. This enables the actor to bring their own imagination to the creation of the character, and avoid being influenced by previous productions, editors, or lazy writing on the playwright's part.

Too often one has seen a young actor rehearse in some peculiar way, who when asked what on earth they think they are acting reply, "It says here *dreamily*." Cross that out, she will suggest, and find out what the line really means in the text, and not try to behave *dreamily* as some editor has suggested..

Another of her most sensible mantras is to ask for long, deep research into the time and place of the play. In *The Anatomy of a Choice* she concentrates on Tennessee Williams' *A Streetcar Named Desire*, asking the actor to thoroughly research the period, the district, the type of housing, the rooms in which the play takes place.

In this day and age she suggests use of the Internet so the actor can see, print, and keep pictures of all of the above, and of the kind of clothes, objects, or props that help to bring the character to life. Most sensible.

She asks the actor to investigate and define every objective in active language of each character in the play. In *Streetcar* she even goes deeply into the scene where the Newpaper Boy comes to collect money, and discusses the objectives, obstacles, and actions of both Blanche and the Boy. She suggests the actors meet outside rehearsal so that they can agree on the same objectives, and not be playing at odds with each other.

At the end of the book she sensibly includes a copy of scene ten from *Streetcar*, the rape/seduction scene between Blanche and Stanley, suggesting their options, tactics, and objectives. Obviously influenced by the teachings of the great Stanislavski, she asks the actor to discover all of the names a character may have; married status; age; their parents and the relationships they may have—or have had—with them and with any siblings; likes; dislikes—in other words, everything and anything that can be discovered about the character to enable the actor to bring it to true theatrical life.

In short, *The Anatomy of a Choice* asks (demands!) that an actor go about his or her work with the seriousness that the art deserves. Unfortunately, there is still an attitude amongst some young beginning actors that all they have to do is to show up to some rehearsals, roughly learn their lines, and have some fun. *The Anatomy of a Choice* certainly puts the lie to that.

At the same time it points the way, leading the actor to the real *fun*: the thrill, the joy of creation—the wonderful elation that comes with true acting. Maura Vaughn will show the actor how to build a wonderful character based on imaginative truth and hard work.

Her book is a gift to any actor of any age. Read it. Any actor will certainly learn a lot.

Jeremy Geidt

Senior Actor, American Repertory Theater

Lecturer in Drama, Harvard College

INTRODUCTION

Artists are magical helpers. Evoking symbols and motifs that connect us to our deeper selves, they can help us along the heroic journey of our own lives.

—Joseph Campbell, *Pathways to Bliss*[1]

INTRODUCTION

ACTING IS MUCH LIKE A PUZZLE: once all of the pieces are in place, they fit easily. Leave even one piece out, and the puzzle is incomplete. Force one into place, and the puzzle no longer reveals a clear picture. So it is with acting. In order to be free to be creative, impulsive, and daring, an actor must look at the information in the script. An artist mines the text first, and then creates art.

An actor must first understand how to unravel the play before making any assumptions about a character. It is too easy before fully reading the play to impose limits and decide that a character would never behave in a certain way. It is too easy to look at the character not from the perspective of the facts in the script but from a similarity to one's own life or to other characters that one has seen or played, and so merely to re-create oneself within the play rather than to build the character.

To be a great artist one must love the art and be willing to do many hours of hard work. Anyone can learn to act, but few are real artists. To be among the few who create art, know that it takes patience and perseverance, not because it is such an uncertain and competitive field, but because art comes from great personal toil.

I have called this book *The Anatomy of a Choice* because it is a guide to finding the different pieces of a character and a map to assembling those pieces—or **choices**—together. Working through a play provides the opportunity to make a long series of conscious choices about how to approach a role. These choices need to be in place before going into rehearsal, even though the process of rehearsing with a director and fellow actors will alter many of them. This book will help make those initial choices.

In this guide to breaking down a script, I have quoted liberally from many great acting teachers—particularly Constantin Stanislavski. Directing and teaching during the late nineteenth and early twentieth centuries, he developed a psychological style of acting that transformed the theatre. He is the father of modern acting, and much of what I write about in these pages comes from him. Many of the quotes that are not his come from teachers who were either directly or indirectly Stanislavski's disciples. These are the great acting teachers of modern theatre. I have supplied a list of many of the best books written about acting in the bibliography at the end of the book.

I have also included journal entries from some of my own students, sharing observations that they made as they struggled with some of the more difficult and exciting techniques that belong to text analysis.

This book lays out how to pull the clues necessary from the text to make the most active choices from which to act. Along the way an individual mapping process develops for the actor. When an actor doesn't know how the process works, he or she creates the character by chance, or worse simply endures the rehearsals until the real fun begins: performance. An actor must develop a personal language that clarifies the understanding of creating a role. The artist must be able to able to name his or her process. Strive to be an artist.

Breaking down a creative process is a wonderful challenge, daunting at the best of times, and imperfect at the worst. Think of this as an outline. There are few absolutes to mining a text, and those are these: take the time to find all of the clues, continue to read the script and reevaluate those choices, and believe that the character must want something so badly that he or she is willing to kill to get it. This book is a way to find the actor's journey, to discover what feeds an artist, what comes easily, what requires more diligence, and what makes one's approach to a role unique.

Acting is a collaborative art form. Some of my students accuse me of making it into a contact sport. In many ways it is. Without the other person or people on stage, there is no one to connect to. A good actor always knows to whom he or she is talking and what he or she wants. An artist wants something from the other person on stage even when that other person is another part of themselves, the gods, or the audience.

Acting is joyous. Make sure all of the equipment is in place and in good working order. Make sure the preparation for this incredible feat is complete, and then build the character piece by piece until everything comes together and the audience gets to witness the art.

CHAPTER ONE

THE FIRST WORD

The rehearsal merely clarifies the problems that an actor needs to work on at home.

Constantin Stanislavski, *Building a Character*[1]

- The First Word—Bringing the play to life

- Things you'll need

The First Word

EVERY GREAT ACTOR spends as many hours or more analyzing a script outside of rehearsal as rehearsing. This book will provide some of the tools that those actors use to create a character, prepare for rehearsal, and evaluate their work. Every actor has studied, continues to study, and is in constant pursuit of the ever-elusive nature of this craft. There are many different approaches to developing the craft of acting. Each approach or technique has a common denominator: they are all giving the student a means with which to bring the play to life. Before starting out on this journey, an actor must be clear about all the aspects that make up the story. Why would a great actor spend so much time reading and re-reading a script? To ensure that no detail is overlooked, that no choice is left unmade, that no action is underused. In short, to make sure the actor knows where to go and what to do.

Text work is detective work. It is a rare rehearsal process that allows the playwright to discuss with the actors why a character takes a particular action or speaks a particular sentence. But in order to embody the character fully, the actor must know *why* and *what*. Why does this character do the things this character does? What makes this character act in such a way? The actor cannot act what he or she cannot clearly understand. Don't be stingy. Spend the time to get to know the play inside and out.

All great performances have two phases of preparation: breaking down the text and building the character outside of rehearsal; and putting that textual analysis to the test in rehearsal. The amazing thing about text work is that once rehearsal begins, the actor must let go of all of the hours spent exploring, trust that all the work will be there, and focus one hundred percent on affecting the other characters in the play. It is reasonable, at this point, to question the choice of spending time pouring over the script if, in the end, everything comes down to affecting the other actors and being affected by them. Why spend the time breaking down the text? Why not just walk into rehearsal and act the scene from whatever impulses arise in the first place?

There may be some actors who instinctively know what the playwright is saying, what their character wants, and what the most active, interesting way to go about bringing this to the stage might be without spending any time on the text, but I do not know any. I have never heard of a stage artist who does no text work. Any actors who say that they never do any work on their scripts are either lying or are simply not very good.

The reason to spend the hours reading and rereading the play, pulling the clues from the dialogue, and trying different ways to get what the character wants, is to open up the life of the play to the imagination, to the intellect, and to the soul. Find the most fascinating way—not the most obvious way—to play this character. Find a way that no one else can duplicate, that no one else can do—not the way any person with little talent and no training can find to portray the complexity that is any character. Put a stamp on this character forever so that every time those who were lucky enough to see the production, read the play, see the play, or think of this play, they think of what you brought to the role.

That is what all great actors do: they make the role their own. Be patient, do the work, don't skip over the steps that are frustrating or make less sense the first time around, and take the time to study the craft of acting.

Research the playwright: find out what else he or she has written, what style he or she writes in, and a little bit about his or her background. Knowing basic information about the playwright will help frame the actor's inquiry. An actor should always have the complete picture from which to work.

No book will ever replace a class. Study with as many teachers as possible. Even after finding that one teacher who communicates clearly, one who challenges, nurtures, and inspires, still read, and study other approaches to acting. Every experience, every observation will help build a vocabulary of characters.

The Anatomy of a Choice will teach the actor to read the play carefully, and find all the necessary information to understand the story, and the character's plight. It will teach how to use that information about the story to identify an objective for the character—to choose a reason for the character to travel through this story, a reason so strong, so compelling that the character would die for this reason. The book will help you identify what is in the character's way of achieving that objective. The book will provide a process for establishing actions to play as the character to achieve that goal. The book will explain how to break down the text so that the character is always acting or reacting, affecting or being affected. The book will give an overview of various techniques to use to fully embody a character.

There are also purely practical sections. The character interview worksheet at the end of Chapter 2 is an invaluable aid to bringing the character to life. The list of tactics a character might use to affect the other characters on stage is a great way to get the scene moving. The rehearsal journal guidelines will keep the actor on track, balancing text work with effective use of rehearsal time, and the troubleshooting section will come to rescue when all else seems to fail.

This book is a great tool—use it.

> *To play needs much work. But when we experience the work as play,*
>
> *then it is not work anymore. A play is play.*
>
> Peter Brook, *The Empty Space*[2]

Things you need in order to make this book useful to you:

• a copy of Tennessee Williams's play *A Streetcar Named Desire*

• a copy of any play that you are working on that you can thoroughly deface

• a pencil

• a notebook

• an imagination

• a willingness to take risk

CHAPTER TWO

READING THE PLAY

It is only when we study a play as a whole and can appreciate its overall perspective that we are able to fit the various planes correctly together, make a beautiful arrangement of the component parts, mold them into harmonious and well-rounded forms, in terms of words.
Constantin Stanislavski, *Building a Character*[1]

- First Reading—Defining the story

- Second Reading—Defining the event

- Third Reading—Defining the character

READING THE PLAY

First Reading—Defining the Story

READING A TEXT FOR CLUES as to how to approach the character is an essential skill for an actor. The actor must unearth all of the detail that makes up the fabric of a character's life and psychology in order to understand what motivates this character. It is difficult not to become fascinated by those aspects of a character that echo one's own life and skim over those parts that are less similar. It is incredibly easy to become so wrapped up in the complexity of the story, so taken by the plight of the character, that the road signs that the playwright left for the actor to follow are missed.

But herein lies a dilemma: it is essential for actors to be empathetic toward the characters that they are playing, yet actors can never allow their own personalities to dictate the opportunities available to the characters. An actor will read the play the first time through and live every moment with each character: root for them, yell at them, identify with their pain, laugh with them in those moments of joy. But once the actor has fully enjoyed the simple story of the play, he or she must go back and read it again.

Actors are naturally empathetic; why else would they be so interested in transforming themselves into other people? They can easily understand what characters are going through and can almost feel their pain. They enjoy seeing the world from a different perspective, enjoy taking on characters, want to explore new ideas, new cultures, and new feelings. Otherwise, why be an actor? But the mistake many young, wonderfully creative actors make is to read the story of the play, and superimpose their own struggles, desires, needs onto the characters before they have fully investigated what the playwright is grappling with. As Stanislavski said, "Love art in yourself, not yourself in art."[2] Before making any decisions about a text or the roles within, please look carefully at the clues given by the playwright. How can an empathetic person not be so moved be the character that he or she is playing that he or she loses objectivity?

By reading the play. Reading the entire play. Reading the play more than once. Reading the play at least three times.

While reading the play, look carefully at all of the factual information given by the playwright. Extrapolate from the script answers to the questions that make up a character's history. Make bold choices from which to act the role, but make sure those choices are grounded in the reality of the script. Review those bold choices after trying them out in rehearsal and make sure that they are the most active choices, the most effective choices. Affect the other people on stage, and be affected. Read the play, think, read the text again, think once more, feel, and do. Acting is *doing*. The audience cannot see what the actor thinks or feels; the audience can only see what those thoughts and feelings make the actor do. Be an actor.

Every actor needs to read the *whole* play, not just the scene on which he or she is working in class or the eight pages in which the character appears. There are clues on every page of the script. It often seems as if the actor can save him- or herself some time and effort by only reading those sections that he or she is actually going to be working on, but don't be fooled—an actor will have to work five times harder to create a world as rich as the one the playwright has already given, and even then the actor has no guarantee that the reality that he or she has invented is consistent with the one that the other characters from the play are inhabiting. Read the entire script, from *lights up* to *blackout*.

It may seem a bit extreme to read a play through three times, but it is impossible to find out all the necessary information in the first read-through. This chapter divides the reading into three easy steps: read the play to define the story, read the play to define the event, and read the play to define the character.

Each reading allows the actor to gain total familiarity with the text in order to become sensitive to the nuance of the playwright's choice of language: what does the character say, how does the character say it, and why does the character say it? It is very difficult not to get distracted by the story line in any well-written play. The more familiar the actor becomes with the script, the easier it is to see past plot and discover the craft, the inner workings of the playwright's intention. So, read the play. Read it more than once. Read it at least, say, three times.

Read the play to discover the basic story. Take advantage of this one chance to read through the script with fresh eyes. Relish those moments of triumph, despair over those moments of defeat, and laugh at the foibles of each character. While enjoying the give and take of plot, answer as fully as possible those journalistic questions: *Who? What? When? Where? Why?* and *How?*

The Anatomy of a Choice will use *A Streetcar Named Desire* by Tennessee Williams to illustrate how to break down a script step by step. First, read *A Streetcar Named Desire*. Not only is this a brilliantly written script and easily available, but it also provides a variety of opportunities and challenges in terms of text analysis.

Read the play. Don't simply watch the movie. The classic 1951 film is wonderful; Marlon Brando's and Vivian Leigh's performances are superb.[3] However, seeing a movie and reading a play are two different things. A movie is the product of the director's interpretation of the script and the actors' personal choices for those roles. Exciting and creative though they may be, they are someone else's ideas. Each actor wants to find an original, unique portrayal of the character. The actor will read and re-read the play to develop his or her own voice, his or her own esthetic.

After reading the play, write out a synopsis of the basic plot line. If the actor cannot summarize the play in a few sentences, then he or she has not understood the play, and needs to read it through again.

Studying English literature provides a number of ways to analyze the story of a play by defining the protagonist, the antagonist, and the climax of the play. Every actor could probably write an essay on the message inherent in the play, and about the playwright's use of symbolism and imagery. All of this helps give a better understanding of the story and can be incredibly useful, and had the actor not studied this he or she could not move beyond literary analysis into text analysis. Remember: in dramatic terms, from the actor's point of view, a character is never a metaphor. Although the actor can see all of the imagery, the choice of language, and literary allusions as a spectator, in the end, as an actor, he or she can only play the reality that the character actually lives in.

Every character is the protagonist of his or her own story. The character only knows the part of the play that affects him or her. Even so, the actor must mine for clues on every page of the script. In the end each character will see the play very differently.

Here is a plot summary for *A Streetcar Named Desire* from Blanche's point of view:

> *I, Blanche DuBois, am a destitute woman in my thirties. I have come to stay with my younger sister, Stella, and her husband Stanley Kowalski. I have been relieved of my job as a teacher of English because I had an intimate relationship with a young man of seventeen. In addition, the family plantation has been lost to debt. I was once married to a young man, Allan, who shot himself after I caught him having homosexual relations. I hope that Stanley's friend, Mitch, will marry me and give me a place to live, but Stanley succeeds in destroying my chances with Mitch. Tensions between myself and Stanley reach the point of violence, and I am sent to live in an asylum.*

Another actor might write this differently. There is never only one way to see a role. One actor may have added something another actor feels is secondary, and the other actor may have left something out that the first actor feels is essential. How does an actor create a role in a different way from all others who have performed that role before? It is all about how the actor interprets the text.

Choose a character from *A Streetcar Named Desire* and write out a synopsis of the play from that character's point of view.

It needn't be one of the leads. There is a wonderful story that has been bounced around for years about Richard Garrick He played the doctor who appears in the final few minutes of the play in the original stage production with Jessica Tandy and Marlon Brando. They were on a national tour after a long Broadway run, had been on the road for a few months, and the show was a roaring success. Every time the production arrived in a new town, the local radio station would ask the cast to come to be interviewed. After a while the interviews got tiresome, and most of the actors no longer wanted to go, except for Richard Garrick. Garrick loved giving interviews. So, off he went to the local radio station. Everyone knew the show was a smash hit, but no one knew the plot. They would ask him the requisite questions about working with Jessica Tandy and Marlon Brando, about how it was living on the road—and then the question of what the play was about would come up. Garrick, being a good actor, said, "The play is about this doctor. One day, he is called in to rescue this woman, played by Jessica Tandy, and take her away for observation and treatment."

Although his character was only on in the final scene of the play, from his point of view *Streetcar* was indeed a play about a doctor.

You will have to read the play over many times. Only on the rarest occasions can an actor seize the essentials of a new part instantly and be so carried away by it that he can create its whole spirit in one burst of feeling. More often his mind first grasps the text in part, then his emotions are slightly touched, and they stir vague desires.

Constantin Stanislavski, *An Actor Prepares*[4]

Second Reading—Defining the Event

Define what actually happens in the play. When all is done and said, what actually changes? That is the **event** of the play. Define the event of the play, not just from the character's point of view but as the author intended it. Do not simply repeat the synopsis, but identify that central event toward which everything is driven.

In order for an event to happen, something needs to change—not trivial change, but meaningful change. It is a change brought on not just through a coincidence or an act of God, but through the conflict of the play. When Blanche arrives at the home of Stanley and Stella Kowalski, something happens: her arrival changes not just their daily lives, but also how they view the world and each other. Her arrival starts a chain reaction that creates the conflict of the play; it is the resolution of this conflict that is the event of the play. In *A Streetcar Named Desire*, the event of the play is that Blanche is sent away. The event is what the playwright wants the audience to go away pondering.

To find the event, list the plot points discovered in the first read-through. What is the **climax** of the play—that moment after which everything is different? The climax is not always—indeed, is rarely—the event of the play. A climax is a cathartic moment that alters the action of the story. The climax is the narrative pinnacle of the play and does not necessarily involve every character, but the fallout from that moment does affect everyone. It is important to understand the steps that lead up to the inevitable conclusion that is the event because not every character's journey peaks when the action of the play does.

The climax of *A Streetcar Named Desire* can be identified in a number of scenes, depending on through which character's eyes the action is seen. The most obvious choice occurs in scene ten, when Stanley overpowers Blanche. At that moment the power struggle is over; Stanley has won by brute force, and Blanche can barely hold on. That is the climax of the play for Blanche and Stanley—but not for Stella; although she is directly affected by that moment, it is not the climax of the play for her. For her, the climax might be the moment when she decides to go back to Stanley even though he has beaten her. The actor playing Mitch might feel that the climax occurs during his confrontation with Blanche in scene nine. Each of these climaxes is distinct, yet taken together they all lead unavoidably to the same conclusion, and that conclusion is the play's event.

Even so, the *dramatic* climax of *A Streetcar Named Desire* occurs in scene ten, when Stanley and Blanche have their final reckoning. None of the other characters of the play are present or directly involved in this scene, nor do they even know what really occurred. Nonetheless, it is the result of that climactic scene that catapults the play to its inevitable conclusion: that Blanche must leave. That conclusion—the event—affects everyone. Find the actual climax of the play in order to define the event.

To define the event, start by asking, what are the incidents leading up to the play's climax? What is the relationship between that climax and what actually happens at the end of the play? Remember, the event is what actually happens— not just what your character feels, or thinks, or hopes, but what actually happens. The event cannot be something that has meaning for *some* of the characters; it must be the end result for every character.

The event of *A Streetcar Named Desire* is that Blanche is taken away from her sister Stella and her brother-in-law Stanley's home and put into an asylum. Everything that happens in the play leads up to that event, from Stanley's rape to the Mexican Woman's offer of *"Flores para los muertos."*

The reason (or reasons) for the event can be thought of and expressed in different ways depending on the character's point of view. Stanley believes that he has beaten Blanche and sent her packing. Stella believes that Blanche needs to be taken care of, and therefore must be put away (depending on how the actress chooses to portray Stella, she also may have an idea that Stanley had a strong hand in pushing Blanche over the edge). Blanche believes that she has been forced out and is helpless. Look at the secondary characters and ask what they believe: what would Mitch say when told of Blanche's departure? What would Eunice say? Even though the Newspaper Boy is not on stage for the last scene, his approach to his character must come from an understanding of the event of the play.

There cannot be different events for different characters. Everyone must agree on the event of the play and on the event of each scene (finding the scene event will be covered in Chapter Five). Prior to the first rehearsal, the actor and the director should define the event of the play, because, once the event has been established, every choice either pulls the character toward or pushes the character against that inevitable terminus.

There are plays like *Waiting for Godot* by Samuel Beckett where the event seems to be that the play ends where it begins—beware! Look carefully at the each character's journey. Even if they continue on they must go through an ordeal and be altered in some way in order to make the choice to continue along on the same path. The path they are on at the end of the play must be different in some way in order for resolution to occur. Find that difference, and the event has been established. There is an old saying: "You never enter the same river twice." Why? Because the river is always moving, always changing, always different. So it is with the action of a play.

> *The circumstances given by the author of the play must be dug out of each word he has set down. They can determine or condition our conflicts, can supply motivations, and specify the nature of our actions. They are rarely dealt with sufficiently. The imagination of the actor can't really begin to work until he has found them, filled them in, rounded them out, and extended them fully.*
>
> Uta Hagen, *Respect for Acting*[5]

Third Reading—Defining the Character

The third trip through the script is the chance to begin focusing, not on the play as a whole, but on what the playwright has to say about each character.

At this point in the exploration of a text the actor should black out all the unnecessary stage directions. It is time to stop paying attention to unactable suggestions and begin to define the character. Most stage directions come from one of two origins: either they were written down by the playwright before she or he had the benefit of seeing the dialogue brought to life by living actors; or they were written down by the stage manager of the first or most recent production. A well-meaning editor, trying to make it easier for the non-theatre-going, armchair-bound reader to visualize the action, may even have added unnecessary stage directions. None of these embellishments will serve the actor's needs at all.

The directions that should be left in and honored are those that dictate when to enter or to exit, or any stage direction that is directly implied by the text. In scene ten of *Streetcar*, Blanche must break a bottle and threaten Stanley with it; if she doesn't, the rest of scene makes no sense. Throughout the play, there is a lot of discussion about a paper lantern that Mitch helps Blanche put up. The lantern actually does need to go up in order for the characters' lines to make sense, and so paying attention to that stage direction in scene three (*Mitch adusts the lantern*) is important.

Sometimes the stage business that the actors are asked to do—for instance, the poker game—is spelled out carefully in the stage directions. Follow those. They will help synchronize the activity with the action of the scene. Often this is not the case—the playwright will simply write, *They play cards*. In that case, the actors must work hard to marry the action of the stage business to the lines of the scene.

Pay a good deal of homage to the clues a playwright will give through punctuation of the dialogue, or by a direction indicating a pause or a silence. But all of those adverbs and adjectives—*sadly, timidly, joyously, laughing*, etc.—are merely descriptions of the approach or opinion of an actor who played the role in an earlier production or—worse—direction given by a playwright. The playwright gives you ample clues in the dialogue itself; by adding direction, he or she is reaching beyond the page into your rehearsal and limiting the choices of the performer. Do not use the playwright's acting choices; use the playwright's words.

An actor cannot act an adjective or an adverb. When the actor tries, all that he or she gets is a one-level emotion—what professionals call either **playing a mood**, or **indicating**. A better way to say this might be that the actor is pretending to feel something instead of doing something, and is letting generalized emotion take over. A mood will not gain the character anything or affect the other characters on stage. And although the audience can sense a character's mood, they have no idea why the actor has chosen that mood or how that mood alters the play. The audience cannot see the conflict played out between the characters if there is no struggle. Worse, mood-playing tends to lend a paint-by-numbers feel to a performance—every moment is portrayed in a flat, artificial manner, with no sense of spontaneity, originality, or give and take between the actors. Nothing makes an audience start thinking about their own lives and caring less about what is happening on stage faster than to be forced to watch someone play a mood.

The important thing is to keep those stage directions that directly affect the action of the play and discard those that seek to inform the actor about the character's emotional state. So, while uncovering the facts given by the playwright, scratch out all of those adjectives and adverbs—all of those choices made by other people who will never play this role as brilliantly.

Now that the script is void of what isn't needed, write out all of the given circumstances that *are* needed. Given circumstances (sometimes called simply **givens**) are all of those facts that the play lays out about the character: those that are explicitly stated, those that are implied, and those that the actor is able to ferret out through inference and deduction.

Read the play from one character's point of view. What do other characters say about that role? What does this character say about the other characters in the play? How much biographical information can be extracted from the text? In other words, what are the given circumstances?

Given circumstances are the pieces of information provided in the text about the life of the play. Don't settle for saying that this character lives in the United States. Find out exactly where in the United States, right down to the street address if possible. The more specific the actor is, the more specific he or she will be when acting the role. Specificity is key to all art forms.

Now, write out all of the information actually found stated in the script concerning this one particular character. Write out what the other characters say about that character. Write out what that character says about him- or herself. Write out what this character says about others. Write out any factual information you can.

Biographical Information

Once the actor begins to do any biographical work, he or she must write everything in the first person. Thinking autobiographically helps to identify with the character more deeply. It triggers the imagination and the emotions. It removes the distance between the actor and this creation he or she must breathe life into. From now on the actor should no longer think of the character in the third person.

Now it is time to interview the character. Answer the following questions:

- *What is my full name (including maiden name, confirmation name, and any nicknames you may have acquired)?*

- *How old am I?*

- *Am I married or single? Divorced? Widowed? How often? What are/were their names, ages, and occupations?*

- *Are my parents living or dead? What are/were their names? What is/was my relationship with them?*

- *Do I have siblings? What are/were their names? If they are alive, where do they live now? What is my relationship to each of them? Where am I in the family structure (i.e.: eldest, middle, or youngest)?*

- *Do I have children? How many? What are their ages? Names? Genders?*

- *Where did I grow up? How did I grow up?*

- *How did I happen to come to the location where I begin the play?*

- *What level of education do I have? Was I a successful student?*

- *What is my romantic history?*

- *What do I do for a living? What brought me to that career? Have I had other careers? Why did I change jobs? How do I feel about my job?*

- *How successful am I? What were my expectations and those of the people around me? Have I met those expectations?*

- *What are my favorite activities/hobbies?*

Note that some of these questions can be answered in a sentence or two, but many of them can take up pages. The point, in writing out this information, is to gather rich content to use to make bold acting choices, not to craft prize-winning prose. Don't worry about style. In all likelihood, no one else is going to see any of this writing. They will, however, see its benefits in a richly nuanced performance.

Note, too, that some of these questions may depend upon some of the historical and cultural research called for in the following section. Answer them as fully as possible—always try to honor the norms of the time, and circumstances in which the play is set. Don't simply decide that Stanley's favorite activity is playing video games—a form of entertainment that didn't exist until thirty-five years or so after *Streetcar* was written.

Once all of the information explicitly stated in the script has been listed, begin to fill in the blanks with information that can be inferred. For example, Mitch never mentions his age but does say that he lives with his aging mother, that he is a contemporary of Stanley's, and that he is slightly "past his prime." Use this information to figure out how old Mitch is. Make a choice and build on it. Like a house of cards, the stronger the piece (that is, the choice), the higher the tower will reach.

Recognize that these questions are a jumping-off point. Some of them will be easy to answer; some will need research, and will have to be written about in great detail. Each character will demand that the actor focus more on some of the questions and less on others. As the actor develops a craft as an actor, he or she will identify those circumstances that have the most resonance with him or her as an artist, and will develop his or her own list of givens.

Historical Information

Find out as much as you can about the time period and the place in which the play is set, even if that time is the present! The actor must not assume that he or she knows all about a specific time period or setting simply because he or she may have a vague idea from a high school history class about the time—say, following World War II—or that he or she once saw a film that took place in

New Orleans. Go do the research. Find a copy of a newspaper from the time and place in which the play is set, or some historical accounts. Find memoirs, diaries, or letters written by people who lived when and where the character did. Pictures are an invaluable aid here as well.

Here are some important questions to answer:

- *In what year is the play taking place? What is happening in the world during this time? (Note: You should do this work even if the play is set in the present.)*

- *In what season, month, day, and hour does each scene take place? (Note: You should probably coordinate some of these choices with your director and fellow actors if they are not explicitly defined in the script.)*

- *What is the weather generally like during the time in which the play is set? What is the actual weather? Is the weather in any way different from normal? Does the weather affect my behavior?*

- *In what country does the play take place? What region/town/city? Describe the surroundings—get pictures from the place and time period if you can.*

- *What is happening in that place during the time in which the play is set?*

The library is a wonderful place to answer questions; know their resources well. Know the librarian personally. Bringing cookies for the library staff will make them even more willing to be of assistance to find that crucial but rather obscure piece of information central to the role. A simple *please* and *thank you* works magic as well.

The Internet is another place to gain information. The following is a short list of some Internet sites to try:

- *About.com (http://www.about.com) is a great web site for doing the kind of historical and cultural research that an actor needs because it is human-digested; it is a site made up of pages hosted by specialists in particular areas of knowledge.*

- *Library of Congress: American Memory (http://memory.loc.gov/ammem/collections/finder.html) Scroll down to browse via a timeline.*

- *Best of History (http://www.besthistorysites.net). Scroll down the list on the left to browse by period.*

- *Librarian's Index to the Internet
  (http://lii.org/search/file/history_united_states) An annotated list of
  good sites compiled by librarians.*

Other places to do research are museums, universities, and historical societies.

All of this research will give a deeper perspective into the role. Write all of this information down. Make choices that seem to fit with both the script and the research. Be as specific as possible. The actor must not leave the search for information at "*A Street Car Named Desire* takes place in the South." The actor must search until he or she knows that the play takes place in the ground floor apartment of a two-story house: 632 Elysian Fields, in New Orleans. Then the next step for the actor is to try to find out exactly what that area looked like in 1947.

Get a time line of events and trends of the period of time and the area in which the play is set:

- *What is the dominant political/philosophical/cultural movement at the
  time of the play? What are the main counter-movements? Where do
  your sympathies lie?*

- *What is the popular music of the time? What is my favorite music?*

- *Who are the most prominent artists? What art do I love?*

- *What is everyone reading? If I read, what is my favorite book?*

- *How do people amuse themselves? What is my favorite form of
  entertainment?*

- *If it exists, what is the most popular form of mass entertainment (eg,
  theatre, radio, film, television)? What is my favorite show?*

- *What do they eat? Drink? What is my favorite meal?*

- *What is the currency, the average wage, and what do everyday items
  cost? What do I earn? Do I have discretionary income (i.e., spending
  money)?*

- *How do people get from one place to another? Have I traveled?*

- *What are the conditions of the landscape?*

- *What do they wear (style), and what is the clothing made from (textile)?
  Who makes the clothing? How do they put it on? What do I usually
  wear?*

• *With what do they adorn themselves? What sort of adornment (i.e.,
  jewelry, decorations) do I usually wear, if any?*

There is a given circumstances worksheet at the end of this chapter that
recapitulates the questions asked above. That list of questions is by no means
complete. There may be other questions that are peculiar to the script or
character. Never limit the options; keep finding more detail, always ask more
questions. When making choices that affect the other characters in the play—
such as date, place, or family history—find the time to coordinate the research
with the other cast members.

Recognize that the artists who design the costumes, sets, and props are
doing the same kind of research. It is their work that will do much to establish
the world of the play for the audience. That doesn't mean that the actor should
rely entirely on the work the designers have done. It is essential to be well
informed of the historical givens before dress rehearsals. If a play is set in
eighteenth-century France, for example, it is helpful to know that upper-, and
upper-middle-class men wore corsets, and high heels—so the actor shouldn't
expect the character to be able to slouch without falling over.

If the costume designer's information or choices vary from the choices that
the actor has made based on careful research, it is wise to consider deferring to
their artistic vision before playing the "this character would never do/wear/use
that" card. Feel free to ask questions, but remember that the designers are also
collaborators and deserve as much respect as fellow actors and the director. It
never pays to hurt the feelings of people who have it in their power to make the
performer look bad.

Reading the play at least three times doesn't seem quite so outlandish now,
does it? A good actor knows why it is essential to know the script well. A good
actor knows how to make bold, clear, and active choices. Live, drink, eat, and
breathe this play. And please feel free to read it many more times than just three.

On integrating historical research into your performance:
*How can I react to something that I don't even understand? So I need to know
that if a man entered a room and didn't bow, he was assuming familiarity. And
then, on stage, I can decide whether or not I am comfortable with that
familiarity.*
*This is where the given circumstances come in. If we had done them completely
enough, we (or I) would have known that in eighteenth-century French society,
you either bowed or kissed a lady's hand upon entering a room.*
*So, if we do our given circumstances, then we understand our backdrop, and
we understand the rules of the game. If we understand the rules of the game,
then we can play. So today I guess that I have found a reason for given
circumstances.*
Molly Hester, from her rehearsal journal

Character Interview Worksheet

Answer the following questions from the character's point of view as fully as possible. All of the answers require a great deal of detail. Record all of the facts; fill in the entire picture. The more detailed the answers, the more the given circumstances become a tool in achieving the character's objective, and the more the character comes to life. As answers create new questions, be willing to investigate beyond this starting point.

Biographical Information

- *What is my full name (including your maiden name, confirmation name, and any nicknames you may have acquired) ?*

- *How old am I?*

- *Am I married or single? Divorced? Widowed? How often? What are/were their names, ages, occupations?*

- *Are my parents living or dead? What are/were their names? What is/was my relationship with them?*

- *Do I have siblings? What are/were their names? If they are alive, where do they live now? What is my relationship to each of them? Where am I in the family structure (i.e.: eldest, middle, or youngest)?*

- *Do I have children? How many? What are their ages? Names? Genders?*

- *Where did I grow up? How did I grow up?*

- *How did I happen to come to the location where I begin the play?*

- *What level of education do I have? Was I a successful student?*

- *What is my romantic history?*

- *What do I do for a living? What brought me to that career? Have I had other careers? Why did I change jobs? How do I feel about my job?*

- *How successful am I? What were my expectations and those of the people around me? Have I met those expectations?*

- *What are my favorite activities/hobbies?*

Historical Information

- *In what year is the play taking place? What is happening in the world during this time? (Note: You should even do this work if the play is set in the present.)*

- *In what season, month, day, and hour does each scene take place? (Note: You should probably coordinate some of these choices with your director and fellow actors.)*

- *What is the weather generally like during the time in which the play is set? What is the actual weather? Is the weather in any way different from normal? Does the weather affect my behavior?*

- *In what country does the play take place? What region/town/city? Describe the surroundings—get pictures from the time period if you can.*

- *What is happening in that place during the time in which the play is set?*

- *What is the dominant political/philosophical/cultural movement at the time of the play? What are the main counter-movements? Where do your sympathies lie?*

- *What was the popular music of the time? What is my favorite music?*

- *Who were the most prominent artists? What art do I love?*

- *What was everyone reading? If I read, what is my favorite book?*

- *How did people amuse themselves? What is my favorite form of entertainment?*

- *If it exists, what is the most popular form of mass entertainment (e.g., theatre, radio, film, television)? What is my favorite show?*

- *What did they eat? Drink? What is my favorite meal?*

- *What was the currency, the average wage, and what did everyday items cost? What do I earn? Do I have discretionary income (i.e., spending money)?*

- *How did people get from one place to another? Have I traveled?*

- *What were the conditions of the landscape?*

- *What did they wear (style), and what was the clothing made from (textile)? Who made the clothing? How did they put it on? What do I usually wear?*

- *With what did they adorn themselves? What sort of adornment (i.e., jewelry, decorations) do I usually wear, if any?*

Recap:

• After the first read-through:
    Write out a synopsis

• After the second read-through:
    Define the event of the play

• After the third read-through:
    Complete a character interview worksheet

CHAPTER THREE

WHAT DO I WANT?

In a play the whole stream of individual, minor objectives, all the imaginative thoughts, feelings, and actions of an actor, should converge to carry out the super-objective of the plot. The common bond must be so strong that even the most insignificant detail, if it is not related to the super-objective, will stand out as superfluous or wrong.

Constantin Stanislavski, *An Actor Prepares*[1]

- The super-objective: what I want through the whole play

- The scene objective: what I want right now

WHAT DO I WANT?

The Super-objective

WHENEVER THE ACTOR THINKS IN TERMS of the character, it is best to think in the first person; this bridges the divide between the actor and the character. All first person address is from the character's point of view. Text analysis can be broken down into three questions: *What do you want? What's in your way? What are you going to do to get what you want?* The craft of acting lies in being able to answer those questions well, and to put those answers into action.

The first question is the most central. What do you want?

Clearly define, in one declarative statement, what the character wants in the play. This is the character's **super-objective**. Look at what the character does from the beginning of the script to the end. Look at what the character ends up achieving. Look at the title of the play and ask how it relates to the character. These are all clues to finding the super-objective. If the super-objective the actor has chosen changes halfway through the play, then the actor hasn't defined the super-objective clearly enough and must go back to the beginning.

Blanche has come to the Kowalskis not just because she wants to see her sister, but because she has lost her job and her home, and her life has fallen apart. She has nowhere to go. The only person who does not know the truth about Blanche, who still thinks of her as a Southern Belle, is her sister, Stella. Blanche cannot face who she has become or what she has done, Blanche hides from the truth by drinking and by pretending that she is still that young, desirable girl without a past. Blanche needs to rebuild her life but does not know how. As she says at the end of the play, "I have always depended on the kindness of strangers."[2] Blanche needs someone to rescue her from this very difficult dilemma. Blanche's super-objective is to make someone rescue her.

Stanley is smarter than the men around him, but he is stuck in an economic trap that he doesn't have the education to overcome. He is envious of the privilege that his wife and sister-in-law were brought up with. He bridles against the class distinctions that make him lesser-than in his wife's eyes and his own because of his immigrant, working-class birth and lack of material wealth. Stanley wants the respect given to those who have privilege and wealth. Stanley's super-objective is to make people treat him like a king.

Stella grew up in very different circumstances than those she finds herself surrounded by. She has a very different level of education and a very different set of cultural assumptions from her husband and neighbors. She allowed passion rather than sensibility to rule her choice of a mate. Blanche's arrival makes her confront that choice again. Stella wants confirmation that she made the right choice.

What does your character want?

One way to find out is to observe what that character does throughout the play. Look at what the character is doing—at the choices made—for clues as to what the character wants. Blanche wants to be rescued. She finds every opportunity to get assistance from those around her. Within seconds of her first entrance, she has gotten one of her sister's neighbors to run down the street to fetch Stella. She has her pregnant sister run errands for her constantly. In her final line, she begs for the sympathy of the doctor and nurse who have come to take her away: "Whoever you are—I have always depended on the kindness of strangers"[3]

Another clue to the character's super-objective can be found in what the character finally achieves at the end of the play. Stanley wants to be king. Yet Stella and her sister came from a much higher social and financial background than Stanley did. In order to prove that he reigns supreme in his own home, he must destroy the myth of Belle Rêve. Blanche represents Belle Rêve and all of its grandeur to both Stella and Stanley. In order to win, Stanley must destroy Blanche.

One more way of ferreting out the super-objective is to look closely at the title of the play. Consciously or not, the playwright often gives valuable clues into what motivates the characters by the choice of title. Often, completing for the character the sentence *I want _____* (with the title of the play) can give an idea as to the character's super-objective.

What Stella wants is to make sure that she has made the right choice. She wants confirmation that this is the right streetcar—that desire is equal to everything she has left behind. She has turned her back on the elevated, faded world of her family's plantation and chosen to follow Stanley. The morning after Stanley has hit Stella, when Blanche accuses him of being an ape-man, of having let "thousands and thousands of years... pass him right by,"[4] Stella doesn't answer but runs silently to her husband. Once she takes that action, she pulls herself one step further away from her sister. At the end of the play, Stella chooses to believe Stanley's story over Blanche's and lets her sister be taken away by the doctor. Though she may feel guilty about what has happened to her sister, she has chosen to ride that streetcar named Desire, for better or for worse.

Look at the play *Waiting for Godot* by Samuel Beckett, where two tramps spend the entire play discussing the meaning of life while waiting for the arrival of a character who may or may not have promised to meet them: perhaps in the location at which they are waiting—or perhaps not; perhaps on the day that they have arrived there—and perhaps not. What are they doing? Waiting for Godot. What do they want? It makes perfect sense to say, in fact, that what they want is *to wait.*

Every character's super-objective relates directly to the event of the play—the character is either going to be working toward the event or working against it. When a character works toward the event of the play, the road is often a direct one. When a character is working against the event, it is a more upstream battle, and frequently more circuitous. It is essential for the actor to know whether the character's path will be a straightforward charge into battle or encumbered by him or her already being out-flanked and out-numbered.

The actor playing Stanley can argue that all Stanley wants is a return of the peace and quiet that he had before Blanche showed up. However, that choice of super-objective does not take into account the event of the play. If all Stanley wants is peace and quiet, then why must the end result of the play be that his sister-in-law be driven out? Stanley doesn't choose to find Blanche a different place to live, he doesn't encourage Mitch to marry Blanche and get her out of Stanley's house; instead, he has her committed to an insane asylum—he has her put away permanently. The event of the play is a helpful road sign pointing toward the character's over-arcing need. Stanley wants a streetcar named Desire. He wants his world to remain the same, in his control, where he is the best and the brightest and he reigns supreme. Stanley wants to be king.

Write out the character's super-objective. Write the character's super-objective at the top of every page of the script.

All notations made in a script should be made in pencil. Pencil allows the actor to alter these choices at will as he or she gets further into the text, and again once he or she is in rehearsal. An eraser is an actor's best friend.

It does not matter if the character achieves the super-objective through the course of the play; in fact, most often the character will not. Or the character may achieve the objective but not in the manner the character thought possible. Blanche never thought that she would get the help she needs by being committed to a hospital. What matters is that each character is willing to move heaven and earth to get what the character wants. If the actor is not willing to move heaven and earth to get what the character wants, then the audience will be unwilling to give up two-and-one-half hours of their lives to watch the show.

The Scene Objective

Once the actor has defined the super-objective, he or she should look carefully at each scene and define what the character's **objective** is for that scene. Ask what the character is trying to get from someone else on stage in order to achieve their super-objective. Try not to *repeat* the super-objective, but instead find steps *toward* the super-objective. The scene objective is sometimes called your character's **need, movitation, want, or desire.** Each scene objective should lead toward the character's ultimate goal: the super-objective.

If the actor does nothing but repeat the super-objective over and over again in scene after scene, then the performance will take on a very flat tone, where nothing ever builds and everything has the same level of importance. Think of each scene as a step toward the super-objective. Again, it does not matter if the character ever achieves the goal. Making sure that each scene objective is in reaction to the last scene objective will help to shape the journey of the character. This is one of the many reasons that reading the entire play before making any decision is so important.

Start with defining the event for each scene. The event of the scene will not have the same correlation to the event of the play as the scene objective does to the super-objective. But the scene event, just like the event of the play, must be the same for every character who appears in the scene. Is the character working toward or against the event? Does the event of the scene move the characters closer to or away from the event of the play? Does this event get the character closer to or further from achieving the super-objective? The actor must answer all of these questions before he or she can figure out what the character wants in the scene.

The super-objective is the character's innermost need/want/desire. A scene objective, on the other hand, must be in relationship to the other characters in the scene. The character must want something from all of the other characters in the scene.

The character's scene objective must be something the character can get someone else to do; it must be active, it must fill in the blanks in this sentence: *I want you*, (character's name) *to* (verb).

Why must an objective be a verb? Because a verb is active. Acting is a verb; it is the action one character takes to affect the other character.

The key to finding an actable objective is to make sure it is something that the character wants somebody else to do. If the objective does not rely on getting something from another person, then the actor is not thrown into action—it is called *acting* for a reason. When Stanley stands below Eunice and Steve's apartment, bellowing Stella's name, Stanley wants Stella to *come back*. Trying to get her to come back—that's something active, something that affects another character (in fact, that affects every character on stage). That is acting.

The scene objective must also be something the actor can verify; did the character have the desired effect or not? Or, from the character's point of view, did I, Stanley, get Stella to come back—or did I not? The verification must be as specific as possible. The actor cannot verify what someone thinks, or believes, or feels. The actor can only verify what he or she has made the other character do.

This is true for the audience as well. The audience cannot experience what someone thinks, or believes, or feels. The audience can only see what the character does and how those actions make other character react.

It is rare that any character actually achieves the scene objective; if the character did so too easily, there would be little or no conflict in the play, and conflict is what makes a scene dramatic. How many plays or movies are about incredibly happy people who all get along swimmingly and never argue? None, right? Why? Well, what makes a story of interest is watching the struggle. It almost does not matter what the end result is, what matters more is that the audience is carried along with the characters through that struggle to get what the character needs most desperately.

One of the keys to knowing that an objective is a good choice is that the objective must be of central importance to the character. The character must need to achieve this goal or suffer real consequences. Without achieving this objective the character will have to give up a life-long dream, or will have to relinquish the greatest love, or fail miserably, or be powerless and lose control. The character must be willing to die rather than do without this. The closer the actor brings the character's objective to a life-and-death struggle the better. It is of little interest to watch a person struggle to get his/her favorite table at a restaurant. However, if it were essential that he or she get the right table because everyone not sitting at that table was going to be gunned down in the next ten minutes, then the struggle is worth watching.

Wanting to make a better life is not an active objective because this does not necessarily require that the other members of the play engage in this struggle. Blanche does not just want a better life; she needs someone else to create that life for her. The character might want to have a better life by getting another character to agree to matrimony, but the struggle to win that agreement must be fascinating to watch. The more active the objective the more interesting it is to watch the character do something to obtain it. The more clearly the actor defines the character's objective in terms of another character doing something, the better. For this reason *I, Stanley, want you, Stella, to come back* is a stronger objective than *I, Stanley, want you, Stella, to forgive me.* Can Stanley ever be sure that Stella has forgiven him? Maybe, maybe not. The end of the play should leave the audience wondering if Stella will ever forgive Stanley, if their marriage can ever be the same. But Stanley knows irrefutably when Stella has come back to him—and in pursuing that objective, the actor playing Stanley will create a tension that the audience cannot help but be caught up in.

The more easily the actor can verify whether he or she is achieving the character's objective or not, the better. Use an active verb for the objective. Any verb that includes *to be* in it is not active. The actor cannot verify a passive verb—for example, "I want you to be sad." Because one actor cannot feel another actor's feelings, the character cannot ever verify whether the other character is in fact sad or not.

On the other hand, *I, Stanley, want you, Blanche, to cry*—that is verifiable. Stanley can want Blanche to blubber like a baby, to howl loudly, or to throw herself up against the wall. The actor playing Stanley can verify whether he achieves one of these in the scene, or whether he does not.

Note that the specific words and images that the actor uses to state the objective have a huge impact on how he or she will play a scene. Be ruthless in finding the right verb to launch the character's objective into action. If a particular word doesn't quite capture the life-and-death struggle, if it doesn't inspire enough action, then try another one.

Look at the first scene in *A Streetcar Named Desire*. All Blanche wants is to stay with Stella. If she can get invited to stay, then she can work toward being taken care of, rescued.

All Stella wants is for Blanche to accept where Stella lives. If she can get Blanche to accept her choice, then she can stop doubting herself.

All Stanley wants is for Stella and Blanche to defer to him as the man of the house. If he can get them to do this, then he can maintain his status as king.

Stanley wants to be king—as we have seen, that is his super-objective—but he can only be king when he has defeated Blanche. Stella wants confirmation that she has made the right choice, but she can only have that confirmation when her sister, who represents the refinement from which she came, accepts her husband and her life. Blanche wants someone to rescue her, but she can only be rescued when someone forgives her for not living up to that refinement.

Each of these people needs someone else to do something before it is possible to achieve his or her super-objective. Stanley must drive Blanche away or conquer her. Blanche must get Stella to take care of her, and Stella must get Blanche to validate her life. Blanche needs to get Stella to turn away from Stanley and to take care of Blanche, or she needs to seduce Stanley into taking care of her, or she needs to get one of Stanley's friends to take care of her—but somebody needs to take care of this woman.

Use the following sentence as a guide: *I want you,* (character's name), *to* (verb). For example: *I want you, Blanche, to get out of my house. I want you, Stanley, to treat me with respect.*

Do not be afraid to erase everything and start over. It takes time, thought, and many unsuccessful tries before you can come up with an active objective.

The objective is the axis around which everything else revolves. Once you know what your character wants then you can actively find a way to affect the other character in the play. Acting is all about affecting: cause and effect; acting and reacting.

On pursuing your objective as a contact sport:

I screamed and bit David's wrist. He was sitting on top of me, pinning my hands to the stage, while I kicked and squirmed to no avail. Sprawled out on the other side of the stage lay my scene partner, Derek, with a feisty Liz on top of him. We had been struggling to reach each other while doing the Hamlet *scene for twenty draining minutes, but it looked as though David and Liz were winning.*

Finally, Maura called over the chaos, "David, Liz, come sit down." Panting, I rolled over and looked at the ceiling. Derek was still on his stomach—we didn't have the strength to stand up. "Okay, now do the scene," came Maura's voice again.

"What?" I moaned. "I can't. I can't even breathe."

"There's no way in hell I'm getting up right now, Maura," Derek added.

"Yes, there is. Come on: get up and do the scene."

I reluctantly mustered the strength to stand up, and I looked at Derek, who was on his knees. He was Hamlet, and I was Ophelia. I dropped to my knees in front of him. Maura, David, Liz, and the rest of my acting class were no longer of importance. After twenty minutes of guerrilla warfare on the stage, Hamlet was finally right in front of me, close enough to touch! I reached out to him, and said, "Good, my lord. How does your honor this many a day?" I told him that my father was making me return his love letters, and he denied ever writing them. He said he had never loved me, and I refused to believe him. I grabbed onto him and wouldn't let go, and he tore me off time and again, but I kept coming back to him—I loved him; I needed him. It was all that acting is supposed to be—he did something, and I reacted to him, and then he reacted to me.

We had a connection, we were in the moment, and we were pursuing our objectives.

Of course, I had done all of that before, in different scenes. But now, I was learning something new—giving 100% onstage. Forgetting about who was watching, whether the class period was over, whether we were doing it right or not, and just acting. Just being there with my scene partner.

"To a nunnery, go!" he commanded. The scene was over, and I was in tears. We sat on the edge of the stage for comments. I looked at my classmates, and a wave of heat flushed my cheeks. I had just opened myself up to them—they had seen my raw emotion in the scene, and it was embarrassing. I talked to Maura later about feeling embarrassed, and she said that was the price of doing good work.

Jessica Jacobs, from her rehearsal journal

Recap:

• Carefully define what your character wants in the play (super-
    objective)

• Define what your character wants for each scene (scene
    objective)
    in this form: *I want you (*character*) to (*verb*)*

• Make sure the language you choose is actable (active verb)

• Make sure that the verb you choose is easily verifiable

• Make sure that this is a matter of the utmost importance.

• Make sure each scene objective builds toward your super-
    objective

CHAPTER FOUR

WHAT IS IN MY WAY?

If I know I can achieve my wishes readily without any problem, there is no drama. In tragedy, and comedy, and satire, and farce—in anything that is worthy of the stage-conflict is at the root. Consequently, finding the obstacles to my objectives becomes imperative. I have to look for the crisis, the conflict, the clash of wills—the drama.

Uta Hagen, *Respect for Acting*[1].

What's in my way?

Raising the stakes

WHAT IS IN MY WAY?

Obstacle

THE **OBSTACLE** IS WHAT IS IN THE CHARACTER'S WAY of getting what he or she wants. It can be a person, many people, an outside force; the more formidable the obstacle, the better. Again, the actor must be able to define the obstacle in one simple declarative statement.

The obstacle is important because it gives the actor and the character something to work against. The larger the obstacle, the harder the character has to work to overcome it. The harder the character works, the more the actor does. The more the actor does, the more the audience sees. The more the audience sees, the more they care. If the scene is not of the utmost importance for the character, then it will not be for the audience either.

But how does the actor make sure that the stakes are high enough? If the character has a clear, strong obstacle then the stakes are naturally higher; the bigger the obstacle, the harder the character has to work to get through it, or over it, or around it, and the audience will be as invested in the struggle as the character is. The audience cannot feel what the character feels or think what the character thinks. The audience sees how the character acts. If the character cares enough to go to any length to get what he or she wants, then the audience will care as well.

The best obstacle is one that comes from something beyond the character's control. Blanche cannot control how much Stanley hates and is threatened by her. She can try to get along with him, flatter him, or seduce him, but she cannot change him. And yet she must. In order to achieve her super-objective, she must find a way to affect change in Stanley. He is a formidable obstacle. Stella loves Stanley. Her love for him is what keeps Blanche from getting Stella to do her bidding. In just the same way, Stanley's obstacle with Stella is that Stella loves her sister. None of these obstacles are within the characters' control.

Sometimes an obstacle comes from within the character. When Blanche flirts with the Newspaper Boy, her desire for young flesh is the obstacle. Blanche sees her youth draining away from her, and the way that she keeps that illusion of being young and beautiful is by attracting those who are still young and beautiful; it was this desire that lost Blanche her job and her standing in her community. Blanche wants to control herself, she wants to be safe, but her desire wins out, and she approaches him in a way that is inappropriate for a woman of her station and years. Her inner conflict is so powerful that her obstacle almost wins, and for a moment she fails to control herself. And in that moment the audience sees an entirely different side of Blanche.

This is a great example of how the obstacle can dramatically increase the tension in a scene. If Blanche decided that her objective was that she wanted the young man and her obstacle was that someone might see him, then all she has to do is get him inside the house and she no longer has an obstacle. Blanche does get the young man to step into the apartment; now the actor playing Blanche needs to find another obstacle. As with the objective, if the actor finds he or she has to change the obstacle half way through a scene, he or she has not defined the obstacle well enough.

Let us say that the actor playing Blanche decides that the obstacle is that the Newspaper Boy will not reciprocate her desire. This presupposes that the actor playing the Newspaper Boy agrees with that assumption. What happens when the actor playing the Newspaper Boy does not agree—what if he were to decide that Blanche seems like a very attractive lady? Then you have a train wreck. Even if the other actor made the same decision—that he is not interested in Blanche—the scene has a flat quality to it. All that the actor playing Blanche can do is continue to find ways to offer herself to the Newspaper Boy and to be rejected. All that the actor playing the Newspaper Boy can do is to find ways to thwart Blanche's overtures of desire. It goes around and around and around.

Any actor who has done improvisation knows how it feels to be in an improv that gets stuck in what is called the Yes/No game. *Yes, you did! No, I did not. Yes, you did! No! I did not.* Until someone breaks the cycle, the improvisation spins itself into absolute, excruciating boredom.

Instead, the actor playing Blanche should try as hard as she can to control herself and not be able to; then there are many layers, many possibilities. Instead, have the young man want to get full payment for the newspapers quickly, but choose the obstacle of being inexplicably drawn to this woman. Blanche knows that she must not let down her guard and be caught seducing this sweet young thing. She must control herself—but how? The young man is frightened and wants to get away, but he is caught in a web of desire and fights to free himself. The obstacle must not be easy to overcome.

The Newspaper Boy wants to collect his money. He needs to keep his job; the way he keeps his job is collecting the money that is due. He meets an affluent-looking woman and thinks that perhaps she can pay the Kowalskis' bill. He seeks to charm her, in order to get the money. Immediately, he finds himself embroiled in an inner conflict. He finds himself attracted to this older customer, but he needs to maintain a professional attitude and collect the payment that he came for. This young man feels that he is in over his head but does not understand why, nor is he clear how to get back on sure footing. What can he do? What a wonderful role to be able to play, where no matter how or what the character does, he or she is not going to achieve the objective. No matter how hard the character tries, the obstacle will not get any smaller.

The obstacle is what the character works against; it helps to make the objective of the utmost importance, and it helps to shape the scene. The actor should make sure the obstacle gives him or her enough resistance.

On working through the obstacle:
The obstacle is a very useful tool. It creates conflict, increases urgency, raises the stakes, and all that other good stuff that makes pursuing the objective difficult.
Working on the physicality of the Grandpa in The Dining Room *really brought that role to life. Having to deal with the obstacle of his physical limitations, I didn't just* move *like an old man, I had to* think *like one.*
Shawn Boykins, from his rehearsal journal

Recap:

• Make sure your obstacle stands in the way of achieving your
    objective

• Increase your obstacle to raise the stakes as high as you can

• Try to find an obstacle over which you have no control

CHAPTER FIVE

WHAT DO I DO TO GET WHAT I WANT?

"What are you trying to get him to do?" may be asked beat by beat,
scene after scene. It will never wear out.
—William Ball, *A Sense of Direction*[1]

- Beats

- Tactics

- The Pivotal Point

WHAT DO I DO TO GET WHAT I WANT?

Beats

IF ALL THE ACTOR DOES IN A SCENE is pursue an objective single-mindedly, without variation, the scene becomes predictable and monotonous. The actor must break the scene into **beats** and give each beat its own value.

A beat is a section of dialogue or action within a scene in which each character makes a single attempt to affect the other in a specific way. A change in beat means that the scene has gone in a new direction. A beat is a unit of text in which an **offer** has been made by one character and either accepted or rejected by the other.

What is an offer? An offer is any action that the character takes with respect to another character in the scene. It can be a threat, it can be a seduction; but it must be something the character throws out to make the other person on stage do what the character wants. Once the offer has been accepted or rejected, a new offer must be made.

Text work is like nature: it hates a void. Once an actor gains or loses something in a scene, once the struggle, the conflict, the obstacle has been removed, has become insurmountable, or is revealed to be a dead end, another must take its place. This situation is complicated by the fact that both characters are making offers simultaneously, and either accepting or rejecting each other's offer. But that is the action of a scene: an action, a reaction, a different action. Think of it as a cause-and-effect circle. Once there is cause to accept or reject an offer, then there is the effect of accepting or rejecting.

There are many ways to identify a change of beat. If the scene seems to veer in a new direction then there is a beat change. If the level of urgency seems to increase or decrease then there is a beat change. If the language in the scene is much nastier, much friendlier, or much more brittle, then there is a beat change. Sometimes, the playwright will mark a beat change with some lovely stage direction like *silence*, or *pause*, or, obviously, *beat* (and those are stage directions that the actor should choose not to cross out). Look for the places where the objective has run up against the obstacle. That's a beat change, too. These are all clues that something has shifted in the scene. When the scene shifts, the actor must compensate and try a new way of achieving the objective.

When the actor is looking through the script, he or she should draw a nice, heavy line across the page at each beat change. She—or he—should draw it in pencil, since, as with all of these choices, the actor is likely change his or her mind once in rehearsal.

Look carefully at scene ten from *Streetcar Named Desire*, included in an appendix at the end of the book; the beat changes have been marked out with a heavy double slash (*//*). Notice that each time the beat changes, one of the characters has altered the direction of the scene. The objectives remain the same, the obstacles are still firmly in place, but the focus of the scene has shifted.

At the top of the scene, Stanley is talking about his baby; he is in full control because he has the information and Blanche does not. Blanche wants to know where she stands. She asks a very direct question: "Does that mean we are to be alone in here?" Stanley establishes his authority and tells her how it will be, and then he shifts the focus of the scene and comments on her appearance. Stanley knows her appearance is very important to Blanche, and he knows that she has had a rough night, because he orchestrated some of her difficulty. Now he is teasing her, much as a cat does a cornered mouse. The amazing thing is that for the first time in the play Stanley's teasing is more good-natured. His mind is more on the coming of his offspring than it is on Blanche. Why? Because being a father will irrefutably make him the man of the house. He is more secure in his position, and is therefore more inclined to be more good-natured.

Blanche makes the next shift. Stanley comments on her choice of headwear, and Blanche says, "This old relic? Ha-ha! It's only rhinestones." She dismisses it. Maybe she does not want Stanley to again start questioning where the money from Belle Rêve went, or perhaps she is fishing for a compliment, flirting. But in the next line something prompts her to rub Stanley's nose in the difference between how he can afford to live, and how she has and will live. Is it Stanley's reply, "Gosh. I thought it was Tiffany diamonds"? Maybe that was just too demeaning for Blanche under these circumstances. He has said much worse to her at other times in the play. Is it because he begins to remove his shirt, and she is aroused and must keep herself in check, or is it because she is offended by the vulgarity? In each case an offer was made and either accepted or rejected.

Read the scene carefully, and follow the logic of what Blanche and Stanley offer, accept, and reject. Spend the time deciphering what makes each character accept or reject each offer.

Tactics

It may be easier for the actor to determine if there is a beat change if he or she thinks in terms of taking a particular **tactic (or action)**. A tactic is what the actor actually does to get what the character wants—it is the specific way in which the actor goes about achieving the objective from one moment to the next. It is also often called an **action, a verb**, or **an offer**. A tactic, an action, or an offer is really how the actor attempts to overcome an obstacle in order to achieve an objective.

When defining tactics use this simple sentence as a guide: *I want you* (character) to (scene objective verb) *so I am going to* (tactic verb).

The audience understands a character through watching the logic of the character's actions. Tactics are the dialect of character. The particular choices the actor makes will define his or her portrayal of the character for the audience. Like the objective, the best tactics are active verbs, are easily verifiable, and are actions that take the character closer to the scene objective (which in turn takes the character closer to the super-objective).

There is rarely a beat change after a question. Why? Because the offer has been made but has yet to be either accepted or rejected. The only case where a question can be followed by a beat change occurs when the question is either answered silently or answered by a change of subject. In this case, it is not the question that completes the beat, but the silent response. Be careful not to be tricked by language—a beat is not a witty remark or a particularly wonderful put-down. A beat must contain an offer, and have the time either to be taken in or not.

The beat changes when the actor has verified that a particular tactic has either been successful or not. If it has been successful, the actor will build on that success by intensifying his or her approach. If it has been rejected, the actor must employ a different and hopefully more effective tactic. Once the actor makes an offer, then his or her scene partner will accept it by making a complimentary offer or reject it by making an oppositional offer. In either scenario, the actor always takes what he or she is given by the other character, and uses it to his or her best advantage.

In the top of scene ten, the actor playing Stanley might write, "*I want you, Blanche* (character), *to acknowledge me as the man of the house* (scene objective) *so I am going to dominate you* (tactic)." The actor playing Blanche might write, "*I want you, Stanley* (character), *to give me the respect I am due* (scene objective), *so I am going to challenge you* (tactic)." In the next beat, Stanley would write the same objective, but the tactic would change; he might now write, "*...so I am going to tease you.*" Blanche could write, "*...so I am going to impress you.*"

In each beat the actor uses a new, different tactic to get what he or she wants. Why does Stanley go from *dominate* to *tease*? Well, he certainly wins the first round. Blanche does not question his authority. She makes no argument about them being alone in the apartment for the night. Stanley feels he can soften his approach and try a less aggressive way to get her to validate his superiority. Blanche, on the other hand, starts at a serious disadvantage, and loses the first round. How can she continue to challenge him when this is, indeed, his house? She needs to gain ground. She must go from a defensive stance to an offensive one.

Just as the conversation seems to be going her way, Blanche chooses to shift her tactic again from *impressing him* to *suppressing him*. The question is, what prompts her to do so?

Look carefully at scene ten; notice all of the beat changes and the changes in tactic that each character makes.

When choosing a tactic, the actor needs to ask a few questions. Is this character on the offensive or the defensive? Offensive tactics tend to be more positive, lighter tactics. Defensive tactics tend to be less positive, heavier tactics. Ask why the scene has shifted; is the character choosing to move the scene in a different direction, or has the other character shifted this scene? If the scene has shifted because of something the other character has done, the actor needs to know why and how to shift the scene back to his or her advantage. A shift can happen because the character has gotten what he or she wanted out of the last beat. Stanley has succeeded in dominating Blanche, and now the actor needs to work on the next step toward the ultimate goal. A shift might occur because the rug has been pulled out from underneath the character, and the character must regain control. Once Blanche knows Stanley has figured out she is lying about the cruise with Shep Huntley she has to do something fast to gain back some control over the situation. Knowing why the character has moved away from the previous tactic helps the actor be more specific about what next to do. The more specific the actor is, the more effective the actor is at bringing the audience along on the character's journey.

Each scene has a specific shape, and that shape tells the actor a lot about how well each character is progressing toward the final goal. If the actor's tactics accumulate toward the scene objective in a steady climb, then the character is indeed making progress. If the actor's tactics are all over the place and have a chaotic feel to them, then the character is fighting a losing battle and must push harder (either that, or the character is playing games with the other character, as Stanley sometimes does with Blanche).

If the actor finds that he or she is using the same tactic over and over again, then he or she needs to look more carefully at the scene objective, at the beats that he or she has mapped out, and at the obstacle, or at the offer that is being made in a particular beat. One of these is not defined precisely enough.

The tactics that the actor uses tell the audience so much about the character as the story unfolds. In the final beat of scene ten, Blanche tries to use physical force against Stanley. Why? If the actor playing Blanche decides that it is because Blanche is desperately afraid of him then her tactic might be *to annihilate him* or *to frighten him off*. If the actor playing Blanche decides that it is because Blanche wants to arouse Stanley, then her tactic could be *to ensnare him* or *to manipulate him*.

The **choice**—the specific tactic that the actor decides to use—tells the audience a lot about who Blanche is, and the audience then experiences Blanche through the actor's interpretation. The more specific the actor is about why he or she has made the choice, the more of a stamp the actor puts on his or her portrayal of the character. The actor does not bend the will of the character; rather, the actor investigates the character and willingly walks the character's road each show. Think of the work of defining each tactic not as shaping the character but rather as uncovering them. Uncover the character as Michelangelo uncovered his *Prisoners in Stone* from the living marble.

How can the actor tell if the tactic he or she has chosen is the right one? If the choices can affect the actor's scene partner, then he or she is on the right track. If the choice is an attempt to bring the character closer to the event of the scene and of the play, then the actor is on the right track. The reason that actors rehearse as much as they can is so that they can try out all of these tactics and find the precise one for each beat that feels organic—that perfectly fits their choices, as well as those of the other actor and of the director. When the actor can stop thinking in a rehearsal and start doing, then he or she will know the homework that he or she has been doing is working. The end result must be the actor affecting others, and being affected by others. The end result must be the actor taking action, doing.

Once the actor can identify the offer, then he or she knows that there is a beat. Once the actor knows the parameters of the beat, then he or she can define which tactic to take. Once the actor establishes which tactic he or she will take, then real acting can begin. Acting is that moment-to-moment work that takes place between two people on stage who are ready to move heaven and earth to get what they want from each other. It is the cause-and-effect cycle of reacting to an offer made and making an offer—both at once. It is verifying how an offer has been received, dealing with the next offer made, countering that offer, and, always, playing to win.

Here is a list of some wonderfully active verbs to use as tactics. This is by no means an exhaustive list. Notice that each of these words has an inherent physical quality to it.

To defeat	*To seduce*
To manipulate	*To overwhelm*
To dominate	*To conquer*
To punish	*To flatter*
To encourage	*To fortify*
To praise	*To devastate*
To eviscerate	*To annihilate*
To con	*To charm*
To hurt	*To impress*
To suppress	*To build (you) up*
To ensnare	*To tease*
To mock	*To crush*

At any moment in a scene, you never know if you're going to get
kissed or slapped.

Archie Smith, Acting Teacher[2]

Pivotal Point

The **pivotal point** is that moment in the scene where everything begins to move in one direction. Sometimes the shift is in someone's favor. Sometimes the shift is in a certain direction of conversation. Sometimes the shift is in topic. Aristotle defined the perfect ending to a story as being inevitable but unexpected.[3] Look for that moment in the scene when the inevitability reveals itself. The pivotal point is that undeniable moment before which all possibilities were open, and after which the scene tumbles to an almost unavoidable end.

If a tragic character is defined as one who is ruled by a flaw that makes the character follow a certain path, then the pivotal point is that moment when the flaw takes control of the scene.

The pivotal point is an essential part of the event of the scene. Once you have decided what the actual event of the scene is, you should be able to retrace your steps and find that moment when everything shifted in favor of this event. If you do not define the event and the pivotal point in every scene, then you do not know what the shape of the scene is, and if you do not know what the shape of the scene is, then you cannot be fully engaged in the scene. In acting, you must play both the response and the effect. After all, if you are only responding, then you are in reaction to the wonderful text work your partner has done but are not furthering your own character's objective. If you are only affecting the other character, then you are ignoring the wonderful text work that your partner has done and are no longer in the moment. You cannot ever really know how the next moment will unfold until you see what the other character counters with. You must be both prepared—having done all of your text work, having fully investigated the play—and be completely spontaneous and open to whatever impulse the choices your fellow actor has made awaken in you. I never said acting was easy.

Again, look at scene ten. The event of the scene is that Stanley overpowers Blanche physically. It is clear that they are going to have sexual intercourse (with or without her consent), but that happens after the scene ends. Find the moment in the scene where the dialogue shifts toward this event. Where is that one line after which the scene tumbles inevitably into that aggressive embrace?

I would put it at Stanley's line: "Was this before or after the telegram came from the Texas oil millionaire?" Up until this point Stanley has not openly challenged Blanche's story. After this point he strips her of her illusions, then he cuts off any possible escape, and finally he takes her physically. Another actor might decide that the pivotal point occurs once Blanche directly insults Stanley by referring to him as a swine. Yet another actor might argue that the pivotal point is when she breaks the bottle, and tries to beat Stanley at his own game. All of these are viable. The essential thing is that the director and scene partners be in agreement, and that each choice gives the greatest possible engagement between the actors.

Doing the homework provides all of the tools needed to be open and available to whatever comes up on stage. The work of delving into the text allows the actor to react from the character's impulses, not just his or her own.

On the Joy of Tactics

I thought this was one of the best times I've ever had on stage. There were three things that I learned.

The first one was that the key to acting is **affecting someone**. *You can never be up there alone. I now know how tactics fit in. They are focusing or limiting the path of where you want to lead someone. Eventually you want them to end up somewhere, but the tactics are landmarks on the way.*

The second thing that I learned is that affecting people is really, really fun. Maybe it's just because I was in the play with Sean, and I'm comfortable with him. Being this comfortable opens me up to a vast number of possibilities.

The third thing I've learned is that going over each line is really helpful. You can finally understand why they are saying what they are saying, and it gives you a better sense of the character. So tactics are words manifesting actions that represent appeals to the core of a person. Sexual core, intellectual core, compassionate core, whatever— just get that person to **do** *something.*

Molly Hester, from her rehearsal journal

Recap:

• Divide the scene into beats

• Define a tactic for each beat:
   I want you (character) to (scene objective verb), so I'm
   going to (tactic verb)

• Identify the pivotal point of the scene

CHAPTER SIX

CREATING THE WORLD

OF THE CHARACTER

In any form we seek the experience of going beyond what we already know.

Viola Spolin. *Improvisation for the Actor*[1]

- The Magic If—finding the character in yourself

- The moment before and moment after—where am I coming from, and where am I going to?

- Inner Monologue and Subtext—what is going on behind what I say?

- Endowment—creating a relationship to the world of the play

- Stage business and secondary activity—making your actions real

- Secret—finding the hidden center of your character

CREATING THE WORLD OF THE CHARACTER

The Magic If

TO KNOW HOW TO CREATE THE WORLD OF A CHARACTER takes a lifetime of study. There are many wonderful techniques to assist the actor in his or her pursuit of "behaving truthfully under imaginary circumstances."[2] The purpose of this book is to help the actor break down the text before he or she goes into rehearsal. Stepping into the world of the character is a wonderful process—finding out the nuance of each new person the actor not only gets to know really well, but also lives with for a period of time. There is an incredible intimacy between the actor and the character. This next section looks at a few different techniques that will greatly assist the actor in preparing for the rehearsal process. These techniques will ground the actor not merely in the words that the playwright has given, but in the living world of the play.

Again, this is not an exhaustive sector. Nothing can replace the exploration that an actor does in a studio classroom situation. Should any of these exercises inspire, please go and find a teacher who specializes in that technique. Never be afraid to try new approaches to acting. The more the actor open him- or herself to new ideas, the more he or she keeps learning, the richer his or her work as an actor, and the fuller his or her life as a person.

All of those given circumstances that the actor collected while reading the play are essential tools in helping the actor to flesh out the character and to create a believable relationship to the time and place the character lives in. Once the actor has fully investigated the text and the given circumstances and knows his or her character intimately, then he or she is ready to bring him- or herself to the character.

Answer the question, *what would I do if I were in this character's position?* This simple question, known as the **Magic If**, lies at the very center of Stanislavski's acting technique, and transforms the character's wants into action.[3] It is of vital importance that the actor defines the character's position in great detail. Create a character history. Review the given circumstances, both explicitly factual and implied. The actor must make sure he or she has done all of the research for the time period. Before the actor can tuck him- or herself firmly into the shoes of the character, he or she must know exactly what the shoes look like, what they are made of, and how well they fit.

Create a character history for Blanche up until the play begins. The actor must decide: if he or she were in Blanche's shoes what would he or she do? As Blanche stands on the street corner looking for her sister's address, what is she thinking? What is she feeling? What does she need more than anything else? How will she ingratiate herself into the Kowalski's home? What will she do?

What is Stanley's background? Where did Stanley grow up? What was his experience in the war like? Was he recognized or passed over? How does he feel about his job, his marriage, and his neighbors? Coming back from work with his friend Mitch, what is he thinking about? What is he proudest of? What is he most ashamed of? What is he doing?

Before the actor can imagine what he or she would do as the character, the actor needs to know the character's assets and limitations intimately, and the actor needs to have internalized the circumstances in which the character lives.

If the actor cannot imagine acting as the character does, then the actor must find circumstances that *would* cause him or her to make the kinds of choices that the character makes. If the actor playing Stanley is disgusted by the idea of overpowering Blanche, then he or she must find a set of givens that make this choice reasonable—that make it the only choice. The actor must never judge the character.

Likewise, in approaching a role, the actor must never judge him- or herself. Each person is capable of the full range of human behavior. People limit themselves based on how they were raised, and by a personal sense of morality or propriety.

There are circumstances under which each person would make choices that might be beyond the limits of morality or propriety. Perhaps Stanley feels that he must act as he does because of abuse in his own past, or because of something that Mitch has said regarding Blanche, demeaning Stanley's status.

Ask, truthfully and without judgment, *What would make me act as this character is acting?* Then try to find givens for the character that motivate this action. If the choice is the right one, it will resonate with every other choice the actor has made and enrich the characterization.

Looking at the Magic If will take the actor beyond preparation and into rehearsal technique. Please look at the bibliography at the end of this book to study this technique further. It is central to Stanislavski's method, and many great acting teachers have written eloquently on this technique.

Nothing can substitute for the exploration the actor will find in a studio acting class; to study this approach in depth, find a teacher who either specializes in the Method or teaches from the school of Stanislavski.

The Moment Before and the Moment After

Every character must have a life off stage as well as on. It is up to the actor to create the moment before the character comes on stage, so the character isn't entering from a vacuum.

This pre-entrance existence is called **the moment before**.

Let us look at Blanche. Before Blanche makes her first entrance in the play, she has gone through an ordeal. Over the course of the rest of the play, she is kind enough to give us many clues to this ordeal: she has lost her job and left her home town under somewhat scandalous circumstances, she is without financial means, she has lost the family plantation, and she has nowhere else to go. On top of all of these challenges, she has had to travel to the city, find the streetcar, ride the streetcar, find the street, and locate Stella's address. Look carefully at the language that Tennessee Williams uses to give us Blanche's perspective of her surroundings: "Never, never, never in my worst dreams could I picture—Only Poe! Only Mr. Edgar Allen Poe! could do it justice. Out there I suppose is the ghoul-haunted woodland of Weir!"[4]

Blanche has had a difficult time. How different would her entrance be if she sat in a first-class compartment complete with air conditioning, plush chairs, and complimentary beverages? Would she feel so frail, so worn, so overwhelmed by her surroundings? Wouldn't she be in a much better state to handle her dilemma: the surprise at seeing where she is now going to beg to be allowed to stay?

Her journey—and the actor's—started before she walked on stage. Write out what happened to Blanche, what she saw, smelled, heard, and tasted from the moment she got onto that streetcar. Do not write out what she thought and felt. Discovering the character's train of thought and subsequent feelings is the second half of the exercise. First, explore what actually happened to Blanche. Now write out what Blanche is thinking as the events happen. It is easier to double-space the lines when writing out the moment before so that the actor can interject the character's thoughts in a different color. If necessary, the actor can do both halves of the exercise at the same time, but doing the steps separately helps force the actor to be more detailed in both actions and reactions.

Create a moment before for each entrance—even when the actor is on stage as the lights come up or the curtain opens. The character comes from somewhere each time he or she enters the stage, the actor needs to know where the character has come from.

Conversely, each character exits to somewhere, and the actor should know where the character is going, why the character is going there, and what the character expects to find. The character's destination is known as **the moment after**. The actor can use the moment before as a springboard into the scene and the moment after as a way of continuing the life of the character off-stage.

At the end of scene nine, Mitch has confronted Blanche about her past, has said he will not marry her, but, under the circumstances, expects her to have sex with him. Blanche starts to yell, "Fire, fire!" and Mitch runs out of the apartment into the night. Where is he going? Will he return home to his mother? Is he going to a bar? Is he going to find someone to talk to? Who would he go talk to?

In scene ten, Stanley says he knows where Mitch is. Is Stanley lying to Blanche, or has he just left Mitch in the local bar still nursing his rejection? The actor needs to decide where Mitch is going when he exits stage. If the actor playing Mitch thinks that he does meet up with Stanley, then he will want to have a discussion with the actor playing Stanley about what happens when the two characters meet.

Each character comes from somewhere before he or she enters the stage and exits to somewhere when he or she leaves the stage; it is the actor's job to be as clear and as specific as possible about where the character has come from or is going to.

The Inner Monologue and Subtext

The **inner monologue** is a character's constant flow of thoughts throughout a scene. Writing out those thoughts is a wonderful exercise—especially when the character has a long monologue (or another character on stage has a long monologue). It is always helpful to know what the character is thinking. Especially at those times when the character is telling an extended story or making an argument, it is essential to know what the character is thinking— what is going on behind the words.

Look at Blanche's monologue in scene six in which she relates the death of her husband, Allan. This is a memory and, as with all memories, parts of the story have been distorted over time. She tells Mitch this story for a reason—she wants to awaken his chivalry; she wants to be the replacement for the dying mother for whom Mitch has cared so lovingly. Blanche has chosen Mitch to be her savior.

But she is also taken in by her own story. It has haunted her and has been her motivation for so much of what she has done; all of the things she cannot forgive herself for have been done in order to lessen the pain of this memory. The actor playing Blanche—in order to understand the logic in the monologue, in order to be able to maintain connection with her scene partner—must know what the character is thinking as she delivers the monologue. What are the things that Blanche *doesn't* say, the memories and images that she cannot—or will not—share?

What about Mitch? Is he passively listening to this tale of woe? No. He has his own agenda. Mitch wants Blanche to marry him. Mitch is most afraid of losing his mother because then he will have no one to take care of, no reason to get up and go to work each day. In Blanche, he finds a woman of breeding who can keep him from feeling rudderless, someone he can live for. It is essential that the actor playing Mitch know what Mitch is thinking as he listens to this tale unfold.

Too often young actors believe that if the character does not have a line, then the character is not doing anything. Nothing could be further from the truth. The character is always pursuing the objective, in each word, gesture, action, and reaction. Writing out the character's inner monologue can help the actor see those moments when the logic of the piece has eluded him or her. It can help the actor know how to deliver the argument and pursue the objective. It can also help the actor to understand how the character is reacting to what is being said to the character.

Subtext is a specific kind of inner monologue. Subtext can be found when the character is saying one thing and thinking another; modern plays are often rich in subtext. Look at scene nine: before Mitch enters, Blanche is lost in another world, a world that haunts and torments her. Through the entire first part of the scene, the actor playing Blanche needs to know what it is she is thinking, what is playing out in her head. Much of what she is thinking she does not say—consciously chooses not to share with Mitch.

The same can be said for Mitch. The moment he enters, he is thinking things that he is unwilling to put into words. As the scene progresses, he begins to make accusations and corners Blanche—but he never puts the full weight of his thoughts into words. It would be incredibly valuable for the actor if he wrote out all of the things Mitch is not saying (the subtext) and all of the things Mitch is thinking that actually underlie his spoken lines (the inner monologue). Writing out the subtext allows the actor to live in the world of the character more fully, to understand the emotional build of the scene more clearly, and to be more open to being affected by the actions of the other character on stage.

Endowment

The character's world is defined not only by people, but also by the objects the character interacts with. The process of creating a relationship with those objects is called **endowment**.

When the actor endows something, he or she give it meaning not just to the character, but to him- or herself as well. Look at the second scene of *Streetcar*. Blanche has a packet of letters that are so important to her that she says she will burn them simply because Stanley has handled them. They are letters of love to her from Allan, her deceased husband. Endowment helps the actor to make these props more personal. If the actor endows the letters well the audience will know how the letters smell, the memories the letters evoke, how important the letters are. The audience will witness how the actor handles the letters carefully, the way the actor ties the ribbon back around the letters lovingly, and they will know how much these letters mean to the character.

But how can an actor have feelings for a pile of paper that has been stained with tea to look like aging letters and then crumpled so that they seem to have been read and reread? How will the actor endow this pile of paper and transform them into the letters of a long and tragically lost love? As with the Magic If, endowment is something the actor must spend time studying.

The actor playing Blanche should try this. She should take a pile of letters—any pile—and wrap them up in a ribbon. Now, she should look at them. While looking at the letters she should engage her imagination, step into the world of Blanche, and ask herself what is in those letters. She should say, out loud, all the lines Blanche says about the letters. She should go further. She should imagine receiving those letters. She should talk out loud about receiving each letter, about her relationship with Allan that coincided with receiving these letters, about special moments that she spent with Allan that are mentioned in these letters. The actor must create a history with Allan that is intrinsically tied to these scraps of paper. She should allow herself to play out the imagined memory of losing Allan, having nothing but these letters to remember him by. How will she handle these scraps of paper after all of that investigation and investment? She will handle them differently; she will handle them with care.

I was lucky enough to be directed as Mrs. Cratchit in a stage version of *A Christmas Carol* at ACT in San Francisco, by a woman who had a wonderful vision for this play, filled with evocative detail. One of those details was having Tiny Tim's funeral shroud run the width of the stage. Well, the stage was probably sixty feet wide. We did nine or more performances a week, so all of the younger members of the Cratchit family (and there were many) were double-cast, and each had a different schedule. I was never sure, from performance to performance, which young actors were playing my children. The logistics of gathering my brood—as well as that enormous piece of cloth—and preparing to walk on stage made any emotional preparation immediately prior to the entrance impossible. So I had to endow that shroud.

Remember, this is my youngest child's funeral shroud that I am sewing with my own hands. The grief I feel is stitched into each seam. The scene requires me to collect myself as I see the shining faces of my remaining children. In order to collect myself, I had to be near the point of collapse.

I held that enormous length of cloth, I talked to it, I actually sewed some of it, I handled it with care back-stage—I fussed at the children if they gripped it too tightly. When the time came for me to pull it across the sixty-foot stage I wept openly but had to work against that wave of emotion for the sake of my remaining children, huddled together, witnessing my lapse of decorum. My overwhelming sorrow was the obstacle that the director and I had found for this scene, and that shroud, thoroughly endowed, made that obstacle very real and challenging for me.

The actor can endow props, costumes, the set, and even the other characters in the show. The actors playing Blanche and Stella should get together outside of rehearsal and talk, in character, about their childhood. They should reminisce about their favorite holiday or outing, about the favorite gift they received or gave, about what happened when one of them was in trouble with their parents and the other had to bail her out. This is endowing the relationship, filling in the world of the character. Stanley and Stella should go off and talk about their first date, when he asked her to marry him, what their lives were like when they first moved in to Elysian Fields. The actor should stay in character when he or she is endowing the relationship. Afterwards, take the time to acknowledge the exercise has added to the fabric of the character.

Endowment awakens the imagination, and makes it easier for the actor to live in the character's world. It enfolds the actor in the world of the character.

Stage Business and Secondary Activity

Once the actor has made the physical world of the play real for him- or herself, the actor needs to find ways to actually interact with it. This is known as **stage business**. A piece of stage business that is ongoing is called a **secondary activity**.

It has already been established that an audience cannot hear the actor's thoughts or feel the actor's feelings—the audience reacts to what the actor does. How, where, and for what purpose the actor moves on stage is all part of what the actor does. Do not merely cross from one side of the stage to the other for dramatic effect—cross from one side of the stage to the other to get something: a drink, a blunt object, or something necessary to the secondary activity. Cross the stage with purpose: to get a drink before the character's head explodes, because the character is about to say something he or she will deeply regret, because the character is being cornered and has to get out, or because the character wants to corner someone else. Have a reason for crossing the stage. As with everything the actor does on stage, each move should serve the purpose of achieving the character's scene and super-objective.

Secondary activity is a physical action that the actor can continue while otherwise pursuing the objective: sewing, needlepoint, clock repair, shoe polishing, reading, writing a letter, cleaning, folding laundry, dancing, beading, making a martini. If the actor has a secondary activity he or she will have something to go toward when he or she needs to cross the stage.

Secondary activity is a great way to get the actor's body fully engaged in the life of the character. Many young actors don't know what to do with their hands, so how better to combat that than to give themselves something to do? A good secondary activity can be continued for as long as the dialogue requires, will demand some concentration, but can be done without entirely monopolizing the actor's focus.

Once the actor gets adept at pursuing the objective, he or she can use the secondary activity to augment each tactic. As the tensions increase between Stella's husband and her sister, Stella might find it useful to be tidying up constantly around the apartment—picking things up, moving things around, folding laundry, dusting. This gives the actor playing Stella an opportunity to vary her tactics, because so much of what she does is simply to keep both Blanche and Stanley happy.

Sandy Meisner has a wonderful exercise called **independent activity**; he used it in his training to ground actors in the moment, to help them relax and affect their scene partners without self-consciousness. If you look through *Sanford Meisner on Acting*, the wonderful book about his method, you can find more information on this approach.[5]

With a secondary activity, the actor will not only have something to do while he or she is pursuing the objective, but will also have added detailed information about the character and the character's daily life to the play. This is the beginning of creating a physical life—keeping the actor's body fully engaged in the everyday activities of the character.

Secret

Sometimes it is helpful to give the character a **secret**—one that either carries the actor through the play or just through the scene. The point of a secret is to augment the emotional life of the character, to make the character more three-dimensional, more unpredictable, and more human. Every well-written character has a secret.

Stella has a secret in the first scene of the play: her sister does not know that she is pregnant. Blanche goes on and on about how Stella has become a bit plump and must watch it around her hips. Stella knows her weight gain is the result of her pregnancy. But what Stella never shares with anyone is how she feels about being pregnant. Is she a bit afraid? Is she less inclined to take Blanche's side in the end because she now has her own child to protect? Is she feeling so elated that she does not see the warning signs between her sister and her husband until it is too late? Is she concerned about how Stanley will react to the baby? Is she concerned that Stanley will be jealous when the baby comes? Does it bind her to Stanley even more strongly than just her love for him? One secret the actor might choose for Stella is that Stella wants to get Blanche settled somewhere else before the baby is born.

Over the course of the play everyone has to unearth information from Blanche in order to understand her situation. But Blanche has one secret no one must ever know. Blanche is driven by her desires, especially for young men. Mitch has a secret, but we never learn it, and therefore the actor must make a choice: one possibility is that he is afraid of being alone. Stanley secretly desires Blanche, is afraid of her, or is ashamed of what he is able to give his wife—any of those are workable secrets that increase the urgency of his objectives and make his obstacles more daunting. The most important thing about a secret is that the impulse must come from the text, and that it give the actor something to work with or against.

The secret holds many opportunities for an actor. A secret can help an actor endow the plight of the character. If Stanley is ashamed of how little money he makes and where he and his wife live, then each time Blanche comments on their surroundings he is stung that much harder. A secret can help you reconcile the character's given circumstances to the character's actions. If the actor playing Stella cannot imagine ever allowing anyone to take her sister away, then she could give Stella a secret that helps reconcile that choice. If Stella is afraid Blanche will hurt the baby or wants Blanche out of the way before the baby is born, then perhaps the actor can justify turning a blind eye to what is going on when Blanche is being hauled away. Or maybe Stella's secret is that she is afraid of Stanley but needs him even more now that she is going to have a baby. How could she go against him, and risk having herself and her newborn thrown out into the street? A secret can help the actor fuel the character's emotional fire. A secret can add to the urgency of the objective. A secret can add to the weight of the obstacle.

So, how does the actor decide which secret to use? The actor should find one that he or she can justify in the text, one that intrigues the actor, and use it in rehearsal. If the actor finds that having that secret leads to greater connection to the other characters, to more complexity in the relationships among the characters, and to a heightened sense of urgency, then the actor should keep that secret. If the secret seems to have a life of its own and does not add to the play as a whole, then find a new secret. As with all the work the actor does, if any choice does not further the give and take between the characters, then the actor must try something different.

Recap:

• Ask yourself what you would do in the character's place
   (Magic If)

• Ask yourself: where are you coming from, and where are you
   going to? (Moment Before and Moment After)

• Explore what your character is thinking (Inner Monologue and
   Subtext)

• Enrich your relationships to the character's surroundings
   (Endowment)

• Start giving yourself a physical relationship to the world of the
   play (Stage Business and Secondary Activity)

• Find a hidden center for your character (Secret)

CHAPTER SEVEN

INTO REHEARSAL

As you go the way of life, you will see a great chasm.
Jump.
It is not as wide as you think.
—Navajo proverb[1]

- Bringing Choices to Life

- Tools for Rehearsal

- Rehearsal Journal

- Troubleshooting—When Nothing is Working

INTO REHEARSAL

Bringing Choices to Life

NOW THAT THE ACTOR HAS DONE ALL THIS WORK, and the script looks like a war zone, he or she is ready to go into rehearsal.

Start each rehearsal by warming up, physically, mentally, and vocally in the space. The actor must collect him- or herself in order to give one hundred percent to the rehearsal. If he or she wants to be a great actor, then he or she is going to need every nerve fiber that he or she was born with to be available in the rehearsal process. Acting requires an immense amount of concentration and energy. The actor must review the text work, know in which direction the character is heading, and know how the character is going to go about getting what he or she wants.

Then, take a moment to take in the surroundings, look the other actor in the eye, and give each other full license to pursue the characters' objectives with ruthlessness. Everything that happens on that stage occurs between the characters, not between the actors. If the actor can keep everyday life off of the stage and what happens on-stage out of everyday life, then the actor can be open to taking risk. All is fair in love and war, and anything can and will happen in a rehearsal. Once this contract of mutual trust has been forged, the actor can trust in his or her choices, can trust in the choices of his or her fellow actors, and can give over completely to the plight of the character.

Make an offer. Listen. React. Counteract. Few things in life are as intoxicating to watch (or to be) as two actors who are willing to commit fully to the life of a play. Be warned: once the actor can do that, he or she will never want to do anything else.

After each rehearsal (and a little down time), reflect on what worked and what didn't. Where were the surprises? What remained stuck? Where was the focus lost? This is where keeping a journal is an invaluable tool. A journal is a wonderful device for keeping on track. The actor will be able to go back, years later, and look for guidance in his or her old journals about unrelated characters, to help work through certain moments in a play.

The actor cannot be his or her own critic. The actor cannot edit or direct while he or she is in the act of creating. But the actor must be the driving force behind his or her own creative process and must understand how he or she best works. The only way to do this is to set a goal for each day in rehearsal and then to evaluate how things went at the end of the day. Please be generous and gentle. No one ever said acting was easy... but it can be exhilarating, if the actor is willing to do the work—all of the work. The actor must be courageous, take risks—big risks—and embrace what is best about him or her.

Tools for Rehearsal

Before the first rehearsal the actor has already read the play three times. He or she has written out a brief synopsis of the play, written out the event of the play, completed the first draft of the character interview sheet, and defined the character's objectives. The actor has broken the script into beats and found active tactics to pursue. The actor has given the character a strong obstacle to work against in each scene. The actor has a clear view of what the character wants, what is in the character's way, and what the character is going to do to get what the character wants.

In the first rehearsal, some directors have the cast read through the play together. How nice, a reason to read the play for the fourth time! This first read-through as a cast helps to establish a number of important perimeters: that everyone agrees on what the story of the play is, that everyone establishes the event from which to work, that everyone starts the process of developing a work ethic together, and that everyone hears the other members of the ensemble explore their roles. Some directors start the process assuming the actors have all read the play a number of times and do not need to read through the play together. It is important to know ahead of time what the director will do during the first rehearsal so that the actor can come prepared. If the rehearsal schedule does not make this clear, do not be afraid to ask. In any event the actor must come to the first rehearsal having done all of the beginning textual homework.

Note that many of the choices that the actor made before he or she had the opportunity to work with the director and fellow actors are going to change. That's why the actor always writes in pencil. Don't worry—all of the thought that went into those preliminary choices will continue to inform the course of action the actor will take.

Each evening, after rehearsal, the actor should evaluate the text work he or she put to use that day, paying particular attention to the give and take of each scene, what worked, and what felt hollow. Revisit the character's given circumstances—those established in the character history worksheet and elaborated in the rehearsal journal—as a clearer, more solid perspective of the character comes into focus. Throughout the process, the actor will refine and change these basic choices about the character and about the world that the character lives in, and the actor's image of the character and that world will grow richer and more detailed. Determining which given circumstance helps the actor find the needs of the character and the character's objective or helps strengthen the character's obstacle will alter the actor's approach to the role. Outside of rehearsal, the actor needs to allow the internal observer to evaluate what was working, where the lack of commitment tore tiny holes in the connection with fellow actors, and where the character did not want the objective badly enough or did not make it important enough to give the actor an action to play. Using a rehearsal journal will help the actor keep track of successes and of the work still to be done and will free the actor up to do the action work in rehearsal.

Once the actor has evaluated his or her work in rehearsal that day, then he or she will read over the scenes that the cast will be working on in rehearsal the next day. The actor will set goals for the next day's rehearsal based on the previous rehearsals and on the discoveries that the actor continues to make in mining the script, always making sure that each choice is active.

In rehearsal the actor's focus is entirely on affecting and on being affected by the other people on stage. The rehearsal journal will help the actor to keep the outside observer at bay while in rehearsal. While there, the actor's task is to find that cause and effect exchange in each moment. The text work is important to do outside of rehearsal; it will inform everything the actor does in rehearsal, but rehearsal time must be solely about affecting and being affected.

The guidelines below are just those: a guide to help the actor create an actor's rehearsal journal. Use it as a means but not as a static end. The journal is a tool to record and reflect on the process of building a character. Each role will require that the actor use the journal a little bit differently. If the actor playing Stanley believes that his physical surroundings will be less important than his relationship with his wife prior to Blanche's arrival, and much less important than his own physical needs, then that actor's rehearsal journal will reflect that. If the actor playing Blanche believes the physical surroundings touch Blanche deeply, then her actor's rehearsal journal will reflect that.

Rehearsal Journal

The following journal guidelines are fashioned on a ten-week rehearsal period. Should the actor's rehearsal process be longer (oh, rapture!) or shorter (ouch) then adjust the weekly focus; each "week" should take up about ten percent of the entire rehearsal period. Again, because the rehearsal journal is a tool that the actor uses to bridge the gap between him or herself and the character, the language should be in the first person.

Before each rehearsal:

- *Read through the scene and reestablish the following: your objective, your obstacle, and your tactics.*

After each rehearsal:

- *Evaluate your choice of tactics in writing and change what was less effective; keep what worked. Then prepare for the next scene to be rehearsed.*

Week one: beginning text work (prior to your first rehearsal)

In your script:

- *In one simple declarative sentence write the event of the play on the front of your script.*

- *Write your character's super-objective.*

- *For each scene, state the event of the scene in one simple declarative sentence.*

- *For each scene, state your character's objective in one clear, simple sentence in the form "I want you (character) to (verb)."*

- *For each scene, state your character's obstacle in a clear simple sentence.*

- *Break the scene into beats.*

- *State the tactic your character takes in each beat in one clear, simple sentence in the form "I want you (character) to (scene objective verb), so I am going to (tactic verb)."*

In your rehearsal journal:

- *Write out all of your character's given circumstances. Use the Character Interview worksheet (at the end of Chapter 2).*

Week two: relationships

In your rehearsal journal:

- *Write a brief description of each of the relationships your character has in the play. Make sure to start with the background before the play begins, and build on the conflict within each scene.*

- *Write a brief description of the relationships you have with people outside of the play that affect your choices in the play. Make sure to start with the background before the play begins, and build on the conflict within each scene.*

Week three: mapping the journey

In your rehearsal journal:

- Describe the moment before you enter and after you leave stage for each scene.

- Create (using any visual medium) a picture of yourself and of your home. These pictures need to be historically accurate, and will require research.

- Write out your character's journey throughout the show. Create a visual representation of that journey, whether as a storyboard/cartoon, a map, a chart, a game board, a collage, or any other representation that makes sense for you and for your character. Locate each scene on that visual representation.

Week four: character movement and voice work

In your rehearsal journal:

- Choose a method from which to explore your character's movement. Look carefully at age, vocation, and personal tension. Then look at status and repetitive motion. You will add animal work later in the rehearsal.

- Choose a voice for your character based on status, age, and education.

- If you are working with a dialect, write out your dialect over each line in your script. Find movies/television shows/radio shows in your dialect and listen to them each day. Work on speaking in dialect for an hour each day.

- Write journal entries for each level of exploration. Some you will do in rehearsal. The rest you must do on your own time.

Week five: memorization

In your script:

- Have your lines down cold by midway through the rehearsal process.

Week six: reacquainting yourself with your goals

In your script:

- *Review all of your text work, including objectives, obstacles, beats, and tactics. Change any choices that no longer work. Make sure that all of the changes are in your script and/or journal.*

In your rehearsal journal:

- *Review all given circumstances. Do they still work for the character that you've discovered in rehearsal? If possible change or add to any that do not increase the richness of your character's on-stage life. How can you incorporate those changes into your rehearsals?*

Week seven: evaluation number one

In your rehearsal journal:

- *Evaluate your first run-through this week: what worked, what did not work. Write out a detailed prescription for fixing those moments that did not work. Follow through on that prescription, and keep an account of how well that worked.*

- *Write out all notes given and how you addressed each note.*

Week eight: tech prep

In your rehearsal journal:

- *Make a list of all the props you use in the show, where you pick them up, and where you place them after you get off stage. If any prop has a specific significance to your character write a brief description of what that significance is.*

- *Make a list of all your costume pieces, listing in which scenes you wear them. If any costume piece has a specific significance to your character write a brief description of that significance.*

- *Revisit your choices for your character's voice and physicality. Determine where you are letting go of this character's body and voice. How will you incorporate the use of your character's body and voice more specifically?*

- *Evaluate each run through: what worked, what did not work. Write out a detailed prescription for fixing those moments that did not work. Follow through on that prescription, and keep an account of how well that worked.*

Week nine: evaluation number two

In your rehearsal journal:

- *Evaluate each run through this week: what worked, what did not work. Write out a detailed prescription for fixing those moments that did not work. Follow through on that prescription, and keep an account of how well that worked.*

- *Write out all notes given and how you addressed each note.*

Week ten: performance

In your rehearsal journal:

- *Begin a performance journal. Describe your trip to the theater, a bit of dressing room banter, your character's frustrations, laments, successes, and defeats. Always write in the first person.*

- *Keep your performance journal up-to-date with those (actor) choices you have altered, how each dress/performance was different, how the audience affected you and your choices, and how you will fix/add in that information.*

- *Before each performance, write out a specific goal for yourself for that performance.*

- *After each performance, evaluate the goal you gave yourself. Evaluate all prior steps. Where did you feel you were successful, and where would you like to go back into rehearsal and try again?*

Week eleven: evaluation number three

In your rehearsal journal, evaluate your process:

- *How would you approach this role differently next time?*

- *What might you have incorporated earlier on?*

- *What do you wish you had known earlier?*

- *How was your level of commitment?*

- *How willing were you to take risk?*

- *How well did you do all of the out-of-rehearsal work?*

- *How complete is your performance journal?*

- *How did you grow as an actor?*

The Joy of Journals

I went through my first year of breaking down scripts considering the journal process to be overglorified busy work. I myself am not one to analyze myself. I never got used to judging myself because other people do that enough for me. So to sit down after a rehearsal, look back, and critique myself turned out to be very challenging. Couple that with the prejournals where I had to plan my exact approach to the next rehearsal (based on the last rehearsal, of course) and time spent on given circumstances, beats and tactics, and other text work, everything just seemed a worrisome bother that I could do without. Of course I would already say to myself as I ran out of rehearsal, "Yeah, this worked, that didn't," so why waste an extra 10 minutes writing down what I already knew?

What I soon came to realize is that by taking the time to write everything down, I was able to more deeply analyze my performance and my dissection of the role. Now I had to spend ten to fifteen minutes or more thinking about my last rehearsal, as opposed to the forty-five seconds I usually spared for a much shallower analysis of the rehearsal.

As I began to complete the whole journal process (willingly) the analysis became quicker, but I still spent the same amount of time, allowing me to go even deeper. Soon I was able to make adjustments midrehearsal which I wouldn't have able to make in a week's worth of forty-five second sessions. The cycle kept repeating: I learned to analyze quicker, which allowed me to delve deeper into the rehearsal process, only to unlock more realizations about myself and the character, which allowed me to analyze faster and more thoroughly, etc.

While you may write off the journal process now, make sure you give it a test which really uses what it has to offer, because once it gets going, things just get easier and easier.

Jordan Raabe, from his rehearsal journal

Troubleshooting—When Nothing is Working

Go Back to the Beginning

Every actor encounters a point when things are not working onstage. Every actor will have a role that challenges him or her and yet for which he or she just can't crack the code. Every actor, at one time in their career, is cast in a role that is too close to him or herself, and so he or she can't quite give into the less attractive side to the character. Every actor struggles.

Edward Albee, a wonderful playwright, was directing four American one-acts for a European tour. I was lucky enough to be not only a part of the company, but one of the members cast in all four shows. We were in rehearsal for the David Mamet's short piece "All Men Are Whores," and I was having a difficult time finding Patty's motivation. Edward was trying to be helpful and gave me adjectives to aim for: "Be more aggressive, but find her softer side. Look at the words, what images do they evoke? What do the words tell you?" Directors often have a different language from actors, and playwrights-turned-directors have a language understandably steeped in the text. I couldn't translate what he was asking for into an action. I could not find a way to unlock the language and find an objective. So I went through my process over and over and over, but I was still lost. (I am sure that I have mentioned that acting is not easy—rewarding, but not easy)

One night, after rehearsal, I was talking to a fellow actor, and he said, "Sometimes you just have to throw everything out and start again from the beginning—but not from the same beginning, because you can't approach the role from the same direction. Pick a direction—any direction—and see where is takes you."

And so I did. It took a few more rounds of over-and-over-again, but I kept going back to the beginning. Eventually, it grew to be one of the strongest performances I have given.

Another value to finding your process is that you know where the beginning is and know how to start over from a different perspective. Just as each actor will take away something different from this book and have a unique path to each character, so each role will ask that the actor challenge his or her own process, and adjust that journey to the needs of the character.

Reexamination

Always recognize that any challenge that one grapples with is a gift. It's not just that what doesn't kill the actor will make the actor stronger; rather, what doesn't deter the actor raises the actor to a level of brilliance—just as a stronger obstacle makes for a more exciting objective. Sometimes, in spite of all the actor's labor, insight, and creativity, as he or she makes his or her way through the rehearsal process, things just don't work. Don't think of this as a problem, think of it as an opportunity. If there's a wall to bang against, it must be guarding something valuable.

Here are some things the actor can watch for as he or she goes through rehearsal (keeping this reexamination in the first person):

- **Reexamine the play event:** *When you cannot summarize the play in a few sentences, reexamine the event. How does the action of the play resolve itself, and what leads to that resolution?*

- **Reexamine the scene event:** *When you cannot articulate your objective/obstacle in one brief, declarative statement, look at the scene event and pivotal point. How does the event or the pivotal* *point relate to your super-objective? What could you want from one other character that would move you a step closer toward achieving that super-objective but be related to the event of the scene? What obstacle—whether it is in terms of another character, inner conflict, or outer circumstances—could stand in your way of getting what you need?*

- **Strengthen the obstacle:** *When a scene seems flat, one of the first, best ways to increase the tension—to raise the stakes—is to strengthen your obstacle. Remember, the stronger the obstacle, the harder you have to fight against it to achieve what you want.*

- **Go wild with your tactics:** *When you cannot come up with a tactic that works for a beat, start thinking outside the box. Remember, no one is going to read your marked-up script! Find verbs that express actions that you might not feel comfortable expressing out loud—whether they are positive (like* seduce *or* caress*) or negative (like* annihilate*). Start with tactics that seem far too strong, and see where they get you—most likely, making a bold choice will reveal what was missing, so that even if you choose a different tactic, that bold choice will have moved you forward.*

- **Exchange your objective and obstacle:** *When your obstacle constantly overwhelms your objective, consider reversing them, even if only as an experiment. Sometimes, what you think your character is fighting against is actually what he or she most wants, and what the character seems to want is actually what is in the way. In scene nine, perhaps you decided that you as Mitch wanted Blanche to prove Stanley wrong and that your desire for her is in the way, but have found that the scene gets stuck. Try playing her seduction as your objective and Stanley's tales of her hypocrisy as your obstacle. Again, even if this doesn't work, it may reveal information about the scene or your character that allows you to approach the script again with new understanding. .*

- **Find what you don't understand:** *If you can't remember the lines, then you need to go back and investigate the text further. There's something in the text—or in the subtext, the unspoken part of the script—that you don't understand fully.*

- **Use that bad habit as your friend:** *If that habitual tension or bad habit that your acting teacher keeps telling you to get rid of rears its ugly head, then you need to investigate the text further. Habitual tension and other personal physical habits are warning signs that you are generalizing. Go back to the text work and find out what action you are playing.*

- *Listen for what the director really wants: If the director jumps up on stage and he or she is not showing you fight choreography, dance, or the proper method of using a prop, then you need to listen very carefully to find the actable terminology in the instructions. Don't try to reproduce what the director is doing; use that demonstration to help you understand what he or she is looking for. Then you need to investigate the text further.*

Grappling with the character is what makes the process exhilarating, frustrating, and ultimately worthwhile.

Winning the fight will be different with every character. The actor already knows what he or she must do when he or she is in the middle of rehearsal and things are not going well, or, as will happen, is in the middle of performance, and things are not coming together. When the actor is in the belly of the whale, then he or she must connect to the other actor or actors and raise the stakes or change tactics.

Once the actor has left the rehearsal for the nightly challenge of keeping the role fresh in front of an audience, if things are not working then he or she will have the courage to go back to the beginning, and reevaluate all of the choices. Instead of continuing down a path the actor has discovered is not going anywhere, he or she will find the root of the problem and fix it.

Ten Points of Light

The following guidelines were written by a group of students to help them find out what they could do when the scene wasn't working.

Their first instinct was to look to me as the director and ask what was wrong and how to solve the problem. I declined their gracious invitation to do the work for them and so put my own interpretation on their character.

Instead, I challenged them to honor themselves as artists to come up with a list of ways that they could evaluate their process and make sure that they were on the right track.

They each wrote down as many ideas as they could. We then distilled the following outline from everyone's input.

The students decided to call it their *ten points of light* because it brings illumination to that which was not yet brought into focus.

Ten Points of Light:

1.   *Re-read the script*

2.   *Reevaluate your textual choices*

3.   *Reassess your givens*

4.   *Talk with your scene partner about your common givens*

5.   *Find/reevaluate the technique you are using for your character*

6.   *Find an outside inspiration to assist you with building the world of your character*

7.   *Reevaluate your personal commitment to the role*

8.   *Refocus yourself through physical exercise*

9.   *Stop thinking, and just do the scene*

10.   *Throw everything out, and start again*

Text analysis is a free-flowing thing: it is ever-changing even as it has roots in the playwright's story, roots that continue to grow and to nourish. The script is still a living thing. The story the actor tells is not of his or her own making; the actor must pay homage to the playwright's work. But the actor must also breathe life into the character, take the character into his or her heart, and live with that person for however long she or he is privileged enough to perform the role. The actor wants that relationship to be a symbiotic one, not a parasitic one. Never set anything in stone. Allow artistic freedom to keep everything liquid. Never be afraid to go back and ask again the basic questions: What does the character want? What is in the character's way? What is the character going to do to get what he or she wants?

Rehearsal journals are tailor-made to fit each actor. Create a rehearsal journal that supports and challenges the process. If the actor decides after reading the play three times that he or she must jump to finding the body of the character because how the character moves will tell so much more about who they are and what they want, then he or she should honor that impulse.

Rearrange the steps, but give each step its due. Those steps that are less interesting or come less naturally may unlock a part of the role and allow all of the other work to blossom in unforeseen ways. It is not the sequence of steps that is important in the end; it is the amount of investigation that the actor puts into each part that matters. The actor must honor his or her own time, abilities, and passion and still delve deeply into each component that makes up the character.

The Final Word

I am going to end this book with the words of Constantin Stanislavski, the father of modern acting. He said that the purpose of his method was:

1. To make the outward behavior of the performer—gestures, voice, and the rhythm of movements—natural and convincing.

2. To have the actor or actress convey the goals and objectives—the inner needs of a character. Even if all the visible manifestations of a character are mastered, a performance will appear superficial and mechanical without a deep sense of conviction and belief.

3. To make the life of the character onstage not only dynamic but continuous. Some performers tend to emphasize only the high points of a part; in between, the life of the character stops. In real life, however, people do not stop living.

4. To develop a strong sense of ensemble playing with other performers in a scene.[2]

I leave with those words because I want the wisdom to be carefully considered.

All of the great acting teachers and personalities of the theatre are saying the same thing. They want the actor to investigate what the playwright is saying, to make a bold and active choice, and then to give heart, body, and soul to the pursuit of that choice.

Use this book as a tool, a way to pry open the innermost thoughts, intimate secrets, and actions of the character.

Recap:

• Evaluate each rehearsal

• Keep up to date with your rehearsal journal

• Use the troubleshooting list when things aren't working

APPENDIX

THE ANATOMY OF A SCENE

- A STREETCAR NAMED DESIRE

Scene 10

THE ANATOMY OF A SCENE

A Streetcar Named Desire: Scene Ten[1]

*The following is an example of how to break down (or **score**) a scene.*

The choices made are the most obvious or most immediate—while still being active. Every actor will read a scene and the actions of a character differently. This is here as a guide, not as a prescription.

STANLEY:
Super-objective: I want to be king.
Scene objective: I want you, Blanche, to acknowledge that I am the man of the house.
Obstacle: My desire for her.

BLANCHE:
Super-objective: I want to be taken care of.
Scene Objective: I want you, Stanley, to respect me.
Obstacle: My desire for him.

//Beat 1//

> **Stanley's first tactic:** I want you, Blanche, to acknowledge that I am the man of the house so I'm going **to command** you.

> **Blanche's first tactic:** I want you, Stanley, to respect me so I am going **to interrogate** you.

BLANCHE:

How is my sister?

STANLEY:

She is doing okay.

BLANCHE:

And how is the baby?

Stanley's Super-objective: I want to be king.

Stanley's Scene objective: I want you, Blanche, to acknowledge that
    I am the man of the house.

Stanley's Obstacle: My desire for her.

STANLEY:

The baby won't come before morning so they told me to go home and get a little shut-eye.

BLANCHE:

Does that mean we are to be alone in here?

STANLEY:

Yep. Just me and you, Blanche. Unless you got somebody hid under the bed.//

//Beat 2//

Stanley's second tactic: I want you, Blanche, to acknowledge that I

am the man of the house so I'm going **to tease** you.

Blanche's second tactic: I want you, Stanley, to respect me so I am

going **to impress** you.

STANLEY:

What've you got on those fine feathers for?

BLANCHE:

Oh, that's right. You left before my wire came.

STANLEY:

You got a wire?

BLANCHE:

I received a telegram from an old admirer of mine.

STANLEY:

Anything good?

BLANCHE:

I think so. An invitation.

STANLEY:

What to? A fireman's ball?

BLANCHE:

A cruise of the Caribbean on a yacht!

STANLEY:

Well, well. What do you know?

BLANCHE:

I have never been so surprised in my life.

Blanche's Super-objective: I want to be taken care of
Blanche's Scene Objective: I want you, Stanley, to respect me.
Blanche's Obstacle: My desire for him.

STANLEY:
I guess not.

BLANCHE:
It came like a bolt from the blue!

STANLEY:
Who did you say it was from?

BLANCHE:
An old beau of mine.

STANLEY:
The one that give you the white fox-pieces?

BLANCHE:
Mr. Shep Huntleigh. I wore his ATO pin my last year at college. I hadn't seen him again until last Christmas. I ran into him on Biscayne Boulevard. Then-just now-this wire-inviting me on a cruise of the Caribbean! The problem is clothes. I tore into my trunk to see what I have that's suitable for the tropics!

STANLEY:
And come up with that gorgeous diamond tiara?

BLANCHE:
This old relic? Ha-ha! It's only rhinestones.

STANLEY:
Gosh. I thought it was Tiffany diamonds. //

//Beat 3//

Stanley's third tactic: I want you, Blanche, to acknowledge that I am the man of the house so I'm going **to dismiss** you.

Blanche's third tactic: I want you, Stanley, to respect me so I am going **to challenge** you.

STANLEY:
[He unbuttons his shirt.]

BLANCHE:
Well, anyhow, I shall be entertained in style.

STANLEY:
Uhhuh. It goes to show, you never know what is coming.

BLANCHE:
Just when I thought my luck had begun to fail me-

Stanley's Super-objective: I want to be king.
Stanley's Scene objective: I want you, Blanche, to acknowledge that I am the man of the house.
Stanley's Obstacle: My desire for her.

STANLEY:

Into the picture pops this Miami millionaire.

BLANCHE:

This man is not from Miami. This man is from Dallas.

STANLEY:

This man is from Dallas?

BLANCHE:

Yes, this man is from Dallas where gold spouts out of the ground!

STANLEY:

Well, just so he's from somewhere! [He starts removing his shirt.]

BLANCHE:

Close the curtains before you undress any further.

STANLEY:

This is all I'm going to undress right now. //

//Beat 4//

Stanley's fourth tactic: I want you, Blanche, to acknowledge that I am the man of the house so I'm going **to befriend** you.

Blanche's fourth tactic: I want you, Stanley, to respect me so I am going **to insult** you.

STANLEY:

[He rips the sack off a quart beer bottle] Seen a bottle-opener? I used to have a cousin who could open a beer bottle with his teeth. [Pounding the bottle cap on the corner of table] That was his only accomplishment, all he could do- he was just a human bottle-opener. And then one time, at a wedding party, he broke his front teeth off! After that he was so ashamed of himself he used t' sneak out of the house when company came... [The bottle cap pops off, and a geyser of foam shoots up. Stanley laughs, happy, holding up the bottle over his head-] Ha-ha! Rain from heaven! Shall we bury the hatchet and make it a loving-cup? Huh?

BLANCHE:

No, thank you.

STANLEY:

Well, it's a red letter night for us both. You having an oil millionaire and me having a baby.

Blanche's Super-objective: I want to be taken care of
Blanche's Scene Objective: I want you, Stanley, to respect me.
Blanche's Obstacle: My desire for him.

[He goes to the bureau in the bedroom and crouches to remove something from the bottom drawer]//

//Beat 5//

Stanley's fifth tactic: I want you, Blanche, to acknowledge that I am

the man of the house so I'm going **to flirt** with you.

Blanche's fifth tactic: I want you, Stanley, to respect me so I am

going **to flirt** with you.

BLANCHE:
What are you doing in here?

STANLEY:
Here's something I always break out on special occasions like this. The silk pyjamas I wore on my wedding night!

BLANCHE:
Oh.

STANLEY:
When the telephone rings and they say, "You've got a son!" I'll tear this off and wave it like a flag! I guess we are both entitled to put on the dog. //

//Beat 6//

Stanley's sixth tactic: I want you, Blanche, to acknowledge that I

am the man of the house so I'm going **to embarrass** you.

Blanche's sixth tactic: I want you, Stanley, to respect me so I am

going **to reject** you.

BLANCHE:
When I think of how divine it is going to be to have such a thing as privacy once more—I could weep with joy!

STANLEY:
This millionaire from Dallas is not going to interfere with your privacy?

BLANCHE:
It won't be the sort of thing you have in mind. This man is a gentleman, and he respects me. What he wants is my companionship. Having great wealth sometimes makes people lonely! A cultivated woman, a woman of intelligence and breeding, can enrich a man's life—immeasurably! I have those things to offer, and this doesn't take them away. Physical beauty is passing. A transitory

> Stanley's **Super-objective**: I want to be king.
> Stanley's **Scene objective:** I want you, Blanche, to acknowledge that
> I am the man of the house.
> Stanley's **Obstacle:** My desire for her.

possession. But beauty of the mind, and richness of the spirit, and tenderness of the heart—and I have all of those things—aren't taken away, but grow! Increase with the years! How strange that I should be called a destitute woman! When I have all of these treasures locked in my heart. I think of myself as a very, very rich woman! //

//Beat 7//

> Stanley's **seventh tactic**: I want you, Blanche, to acknowledge that I
> am the man of the house so I'm going **to bait** you.
>
> Blanche's **seventh tactic**: I want you, Stanley, to respect me so I am
> going **to attack** you.

BLANCHE:
But I have been foolish—casting my pearls before swine! .

STANLEY:
Swine, huh?

BLANCHE:
Yes, swine! Swine! And I'm thinking not only of you, but of your friend, Mr. Mitchell. He came to see me tonight. He dared to come here in his work-clothes! And to repeat slander to me—vicious stories that he had gotten from you! I handed him his walking papers...

STANLEY:
You did, huh?

BLANCHE:
But then he came back. He returned with a box of roses to beg my forgiveness! He implored my forgiveness. But some things are not forgivable. Deliberate cruelty is not forgivable. It is the one unforgivable thing in my opinion, and it is the one thing of which I have never, never been guilty. And so I told him, I said to him, "Thank you, but it was foolish of me to think that we could ever adapt ourselves to each other. Our ways of life are too different. Our attitudes and our backgrounds are incompatible. We have to be realistic about such things. So farewell, my friend! And let there be no hard feelings..." //

//Beat 8//

> Stanley's **eighth tactic**: I want you, Blanche, to acknowledge that I
> am the man of the house so I'm going **to break** you.

Blanche's Super-objective: I want to be taken care of
Blanche's Scene Objective: I want you, Stanley, to respect me.
Blanche's Obstacle: My desire for him.

Blanche's eighth tactic: I want you, Stanley, to respect me so I am going **to deflect** you.

(PIVOTAL POINT)

STANLEY:
Was this before or after the telegram came from the Texas oil millionaire?

BLANCHE:
What telegram! No! After! As a matter of fact the wire was—came just as—

STANLEY:
As a matter of fact there wasn't no wire at all.

BLANCHE:
Oh, oh!

STANLEY:
There isn't no millionaire! And Mitch didn't come back with roses 'cause I know where he is!

BLANCHE:
Oh!

STANLEY:
There isn't a goddam thing but imagination!

BLANCHE:
Oh!

STANLEY:
And lies, and conceit, and tricks!

BLANCHE:
Oh!

STANLEY:
And look at yourself! Take a look at yourself in that wornout Mardi Gras outfit, rented for fifty cents from some rag-picker! And with the crazy crown on! What queen do you think you are?

BLANCHE:
Oh, God...

STANLEY:
I've been on to you from the start! Not once did you pull any wool over this boy's eyes! You come in here and sprinkle the place with powder and spray perfume and cover the light bulb with a paper lantern, and lo and behold the

Stanley's Super-objective: I want to be king.

Stanley's Scene objective: I want you, Blanche, to acknowledge that
I am the man of the house.

Stanley's Obstacle: My desire for her.

place has turned into Egypt, and you are the Queen of the Nile! Sitting on your
throne and swilling down my liquor! I say Ha! Ha! Do you hear me? Ha-ha-ha!
//

//Beat 9//

Stanley's ninth tactic: I want you, Blanche, to acknowledge that I

am the man of the house so I'm going **to threaten** you.

Blanche's ninth tactic: I want you, Stanley, to respect me so I am

going **to push you away**.

STANLEY:
[He walks into the bedroom.]

BLANCHE:
Don't come in here! [She catches her breath, crosses to the phone and
jiggles the hook. Stanley goes into the bathroom and closes the door.]

BLANCHE:
Operator, operator! Give me long-distance, please... I want to get in touch
with Mr. Shep Huntleigh of Dallas. He's so well-known he doesn't require any
address. Just ask anybody who—Wait!...—No, I couldn't find it right now....
Please understand, I—No! No, wait!... One moment! Someone is—Nothing!
Hold on, please! [She sets the phone down and crosses into the kitchen. Blanche
returns slowly to the phone. She speaks in a hoarse whisper.] Operator!
Operator! Never mind long-distance. Get Western Union. There isn't time to
be—Western—Western Union! Western Union? Yes! I want to—Take down
this message! "In desperate, desperate circumstances! Help me! Caught in a
trap. Caught in—" Oh! [The bathroom door is thrown open, and Stanley comes
out in the brilliant silk pyjamas. He grins at her as he knots the tasseled sash
about his waist. She gasps and backs away from the phone. He stares at her for a
count of ten. Then a clicking becomes audible from the telephone, steady and
rasping.]

STANLEY:
You left th' phone off th' hook. [He crosses to it and sets it back on the
hook. After he has replaced it, he weaves between Blanche and the outer door.]

BLANCHE:
Let me—let me get by you!

STANLEY:
Get by me! Sure. Go ahead. [He moves back a pace in the doorway.]

Blanche's Super-objective: I want to be taken care of
Blanche's Scene Objective: I want you, Stanley, to respect me.
Blanche's Obstacle: My desire for him.

BLANCHE:
You—you stand over there! [She indicates a further position.]

STANLEY:
You got plenty of room to walk by me now.

BLANCHE:
Not with you there! But I've got to get out somehow!

STANLEY:
You think I'll interfere with you? Ha-ha! //

//Beat 10//

Stanley's tenth tactic: I want you, Blanche, to acknowledge that I am the man of the house so I'm going **to humiliate** you.

Blanche's tenth tactic: I want you, Stanley, to respect me so I am going **to fight** you.

STANLEY:
Come to think of it—maybe you wouldn't be bad to—interfere with...
[Blanche moves backward through the door into the bedroom.]

BLANCHE:
Stay back! Don't you come toward me another step, or I'll-

STANLEY:
What?

BLANCHE:
Some awful thing will happen! It will!

STANLEY:
What are you putting on now?
[They are now both inside the bedroom.]

BLANCHE:
I warn you, don't! I'm in danger!
[He takes another step. She smashes a bottle on the table and faces him, clutching the broken top.] //

//Beat 11//

Stanley's eleventh tactic: I want you, Blanche, to acknowledge that I am the man of the house so I'm going **to overpower** you.

Stanley's Super-objective: I want to be king.
Stanley's Scene objective: I want you, Blanche, to acknowledge that
  I am the man of the house.
Stanley's Obstacle: My desire for her.

Blanche's eleventh tactic: I want you, Stanley, to respect me so I am

going **to hurt** you.

STANLEY:

What did you do that for?

BLANCHE:

So I could twist the broken end in your face!

STANLEY:

I bet you would do that!

BLANCHE:

I would! I will if you—

STANLEY:

Oh! So you want some roughhouse! All right, let's have some roughhouse!
[He springs toward her, overturning the table. She cries out and strikes at him
with the bottle top, but he catches her wrist.] //

//Beat 12//

Stanley's twelfth tactic: I want you, Blanche, to acknowledge that I

am the man of the house so I'm going **to annihilate** you.

Blanche's twelfth tactic: I want you, Stanley, to respect me so I am

going **to give in** to you.

STANLEY:

Tiger- tiger! Drop the bottle top! Drop it! We've had this date with each
other from the beginning! [She moans. The bottle top falls. She sinks to her
knees. He picks up her inert figure and carries her to the bed. The hot trumpet
and drums from the Four Deuces sound loudly.]

ACKNOWLEDGEMENTS

Quotation from *Pathways to Bliss: Mythology and Personal Transformation* by Joseph Campbell, copyright ©2004. Reprinted by permission of Joseph Campbell Foundation (jcf.org).

Quotations from *Building a Character*, by Constantine Stanislavski, Translated by Elizabeth Reynolds Hapgood, copyright ©1978. Reprinted by permission of the Copyright Clearance Center.

Quotation from *The Empty Space*, by Peter Brook, copyright ©1968.

Quotations from *An Actor Prepares*, by Constantine Stanislavski, Translated by Elizabeth Reynolds Hapgood, copyright ©1989. Reprinted by permission of the Copyright Clearance Center.

Quotation from *Respect for Acting*, by Uta Hagen with Haskell Frankel. Copyright ©1973, Uta Hagen. Reprinted by arrangement with the Estate of Uta Hagen and the Barbara Hogenson Agency.

Quotation from *Improvisation for the Theater*, by Viola Spolin, copyright ©1996.

Quotation from *A Sense of Direction: Some Observations on the Art of Directing*, by William Ball, copyright ©. Permission Pending.

Quotation from *A Joseph Campbell Companion*, by Joseph Campbell. copyright ©1991; reprinted by permission of Joseph Campbell Foundation (jcf.org).

"Scene Ten" by Tennessee Williams, from *A Streetcar Named Desire*, copyright ©1947 by The University of the South. Reprinted by permission of New Directions Publishing Corp.

"Scene Ten" by Tennessee Williams, from *A Streetcar Named Desire*, copyright ©1947 by The University of the South. Reprinted by permission of George Borchardt, Inc. for the Estate of Tennessee Williams.

Quotations from student acting journals reprinted by permission of Shawn Boykins, Molly Hester, Jessica Jacobs, and Jordan Raabe.

The author thanks Lori Deibel of the Branson School for her assistance in researching and proofreading this book.

This book was edited and designed by David Kudler. The text was set using Times New Roman.

NOTES

Introduction

1. Joseph Campbell, *Pathways to Bliss: Mythology and Personal Transformation*, ed. David Kudler (Novato, California: New World Library, 2004), p. 132.

1. The First Word

1. Constantin Stanislavski, *Building a Character*, trans. Elizabeth Reynolds Hapgood, (New York: Routledge/Theatre Arts Books, 1989), p. 251.

2. Peter Brook, *The Empty Space* (New York: Touchstone, 2005), p. 141.

2. Reading the Play

1. Stanislavski, *Building a Character*, pp. 170–171.

2. *Ibid.*, p. 242.

3. Williams, *A Streetcar Named Desire*, directed by Elia Kazan (Culver City, California: Warner Brothers, 1951).

4. Stanislavski, *An Actor Prepares*, Elizabeth Reynolds Hapgood, trans., (New York: Routledge/Theatre Arts Books, 1989), p. 252.

5. Uta Hagen with Haskel Frankel, *Respect for Acting* (New York: Macmillan Publishing Co., Inc., 1975), p. 158.

3. What Do I Want?

1. Stanislavski, *An Actor Prepares,* p. 271.

2. Williams, *A Streetcar Named Desire* (New York: Signet, 1986), sc. 12.

3. *Ibid.,* sc. 2.

4. What's in My Way?

1. Hagen with Frankel, p.180.

5. What Do I Do to Get What I Want?

1. William Ball, *A Sense of Direction: Some Observations on the Art of Directing* (New York, Drama Book Publishers, 1984), p. 91.

2. Archie Smith, spoken to editor, National Theatre Conservatory, Denver, Colorado, 1985.

NOTES

3. Aristotle, *Poetics*, ch. IX.

6. CREATING THE WORLD OF THE CHARACTER

1. Viola Spolin. *Improvisation for the Actor* (Evanston, Illinois: Northwestern University Press, 1999), p. 16.

2. Sanford Meisner and Dennis Longwell, *Sanford Meisner on Acting*, (New York: Vintage, 1987), p. 13.

3. Stanislavski, *An Actor Prepares*, p. 65.

4. Williams, *Streetcar*, sc.1

5. Meisner and Longwell, pp. 37–42.

7. INTO REHEARSAL

1. As quoted by Joseph Campbell in *A Joseph Campbell Companion: Reflections on the Art of Living*, (New York: HarperCollins Publishers, 1991) p. 26.

2. Stanislavsi, *An Actor Prepares*, p. 271.

APPENDIX. THE ANATOMY OF A SCENE

1. Williams, *Streetcar*, sc.10.

BIBLIOGRAPHY

My copies of these books are dog-eared, but well-loved. I have read them over and over again. Much of my own book was inspired by the wisdom held inside these volumes. Read these books.

As wonderful as books are, they can never take the place of instruction. I have been fortunate enough to have had a number of incredible acting teachers; the teachers who influenced me and my process the most are Nikos Psacharopoulos, Michael Kahn, Michael Howard, and Caymichael Patten.

Adler, Stella, *The Technique of Acting*. Bantam, 1990.

Ball, William, *A Sense of Direction: Some Observations on the Art of Directing*. Drama Publishers, 1984.

Barton, John, *Playing Shakespeare*, 2nd ed. Methuen Drama, 2009.

Brook, Peter, *The Empty Space*. Touchstone, 1995.

— *The Open Door: Thoughts on Acting and Theatre*. Theater Communications Group, 1995.

Caldarone, Maria, and Maggie Lloyd-Williams, *The Actors' Thesaurus*. Drama Publishers, 2004.

Callow, Simon, *Being an Actor*, rev. ed. Picador, 2003.

Campbell, Joseph, *The Hero with a Thousand Faces*, 3rd ed. New World Library, 2008.

— *A Joseph Campbell Companion: Reflections on the Art of Living*. HarperCollins, 1991.

— *Pathways to Bliss: Mythology and Personal Transformation*, edited by David Kudler. New World Library, 2004.

Chaikin, Joseph, *The Presence of the Actor*. Theater Communications Group, 1993.

Chekhov, Michael, *On the Technique of Acting*, rev. ed, edited by Mel Gordon. HarperCollins Publishers, Inc., 1991.

Johnstone, Keith, *Impro: Improvisation and the Theatre*. Theatre Arts Books, 1987.

Hagen, Uta, with Haskel Frankel, *Respect of Acting*. Macmillan Publishing Co., Inc., 1975.

— *A Challenge for the Actor*. Scribner, 1991.

Meisner, Sanford, and Dennis Longwell, *Sanford Meisner On Acting*. Vintage, 1987.

Sher, Anthony, *Year of the King: An Actor's Diary and Sketchbook*. Limelight Editions, 2004.

Smith, Archie. Spoken to editor. National Theatre Conservatory, Denver, Colorado, 1985.

Spolin, Viola, *Improvisation for the Theater,* 3rd ed. Northwestern University Press, 1999.

Stanislavski, Constantin, *An Actor Prepares*, translated by Elizabeth Reynolds Hapgood. Routledge/Theatre Arts Books, 1989.

— *Building a Character*, translated by Elizabeth Reynolds. Routledge/Theatre Arts Books, 1989.

— *Creating a Role*, translated by Elizabeth Reynolds Hapgood. Routledge/Theatre Arts Books, 1989.

— *My Life in Art*, translated by J. J. Robbins. Routledge/Theatre Arts Books, 1996.

Shurtleff, Michael, *Audition: Everything an Actor Needs to Know to Get the Part.* Walker and Company, 2003.

Williams, Tennessee, *A Streecar Named Desire.* Signet, 1986.

— *A Streetcar Named Desire*, directed by Elia Kazan. Warner Brothers, 1951.

INDEX

CPSIA information can be obtained at www.ICGtesting.com
Printed in the USA
BVOW08s1356260716

456821BV00001B/2/P